7 Steps to Revitalizing the Small-town Church

by
PAUL N. HAZELTON

Nazarene Publishing House
Kansas City, Missouri

130170

Contents

Endorsements

Paul Hazelton is a successful pastor of a vital church in the small town. He has described his concepts and methods of ministry in this book. I recommend it to pastors of churches in small towns all across America. It will lift your vision, your spirit, and your sense of fulfillment in ministry.

BILL M. SULLIVAN
Division Director, Church Growth
Church of the Nazarene

The small-town church has a special setting that sets it apart with unique advantages. Rev. Paul Hazelton has identified them and capitalized on them very effectively. Rather than listening to the negative arguments against serving a small church in a small town, he caught a vision that transformed both himself and the people he pastored.

I only wish I had been able to put my hands on such a book when I began my first pastorate. Here are ideas on organizational development and approaches to pastoring that will be referred to frequently. The concepts are basic, and they are applied particularly for the small church.

Rev. Hazelton is a pastor with "church growth eyes." He has an unquenchable desire to make his church an instrument of effective evangelism. The principles he lays out are critically important. The way the author has applied them makes it easy for the reader to learn valuable information for an effective ministry.

WILBUR W. BRANNON
Director, Pastoral Ministries
Church of the Nazarene

Foreword

In this time of emphasis on superchurches, there is somewhat of a neglect of the importance of the smaller church as a vital component of the kingdom of God. Rev. Paul Hazelton has participated in the leadership of several smaller congregations in which there was no growth. He has a basic belief that small churches can grow and can meet a spiritual and social need in the community.

His experience in LaMoure, N.Dak., led him to look into basic principles of reaching people with the gospel of Jesus Christ. He writes, "LaMoure should be an *example* of what God can do in the small-town church and not an *exception*. What God has done here He can do anywhere as His people are obedient to His will."

This book is not only a presentation of church growth principles for a small town but also a presentation of successful plans of action. He urges readers not to resort to excuses as to why a small-town church cannot develop and grow but to "start with the hot coals; work with what you have."

This book endeavors to relieve the negative responses of hopelessness for any small-town congregation and displays attitudes that are positive and methods that are practical.

Rev. Hazelton concludes that "the process for revitalizing the church set forth in these pages is not a theory developed in a sterilized and controlled environment. It is a formula developed in the always-changing world of the small-town church." This book opens opportunities for new hope for small-town churches.

WILLIAM J. PRINCE
General Superintendent

September 1992

Preface

This book contains material used as a 14-week study in our local church and presented in seminars across our district.

The process of revitalization set forth here works not only on paper but also in practice. This is the story of what God is doing in the LaMoure Church of the Nazarene in LaMoure, N.Dak., and how it is being done. This process is now being applied in other churches with great success.

Part I focuses upon a philosophical approach—seven aspects of revitalizing the small-town church. Part II focuses on practical applications—seven steps that implement the task of revitalizing the small-town church.

Do not allow this material to overwhelm you. Rather, accept its components as part of an ongoing process. The various steps outlined in this book were presented as a working plan, taking one step at a time. Although this process has been formulated in a small-town church situation, its principles are applicable to any church anywhere. It is my prayer that this book will be useful to you in the revitalizing of your church.

I

Surveying the Task

1

If It Can Happen There, It Can Happen Anywhere

> *And Jesus said unto them, Because of your unbelief: for verily I say unto you, If ye have faith as a grain of mustard seed, ye shall say unto this mountain, Remove hence to yonder place; and it shall remove; and nothing shall be impossible unto you.*
>
> Matt. 17:20

Sometimes we can know too much for our own good. In December 1987, when I assumed my current position as pastor of the Church of the Nazarene in LaMoure, N.Dak., I believed God could and would build His church in our midst. Had I known then what I know now, it would have taken the wind out of my sails before I ever got started. I might have chosen to sit at home, watching life go past, instead of putting all I am and have into loving people and building the church where I have been planted.

Can small-town churches be revitalized?

In many church growth books, I have found among their pages of inspiration and insight an excuse for failure in situations like ours. C. Peter Wagner, in *Leading Your Church to Growth,* answers the question, "Is it okay not to grow?" by stating that some churches *cannot* grow "because of the social situation. They have a terminal illness. Either their community is changing radically, or, as is the case in some rural areas, it is disappearing. The realistic prognosis is that the church will die. Growth potential is near zero."[1]

Robert H. Schuller talks about the unchurched population of a community in *Your Church Has a Fantastic Future.* He says, "The good news I have for you is that your church—unless it is located in a tiny town in a rural section—is unquestionably surrounded by a vast majority of people who are not committed to any faith, to any religion, to any denomination. That means that there is an enormous potential for your church growth."[2]

If not careful, a reader will come to the conclusion that books like these are not applicable to the pastors and laypersons of the small-town church, and such a one will miss out on the valuable inspiration and insight they afford.

Who would have thought it would happen in LaMoure, N.Dak.? I did not even know there was such a place until one evening in November 1987, when then District Superintendent L. Eugene Plemons called to ask if I would be interested in pastoring this congregation. At that time he did not offer me an opportunity, but a "time of healing" for my ministry. Sometime later a leading pastor on this district said, "It was the common consensus that the best the church in LaMoure could do would be to survive—it would never be a thriving church." Another leading pastor on the district said, "If the Church of the Nazarene can grow in LaMoure, it can grow anywhere!" LaMoure had received bad press throughout the state in recent years as an example of a dying community.

This same defeatist attitude also marked the congregation. Lay leaders in this church recently stated that in

12

1987 LaMoure was a dying church. Several times during my first few months as pastor, people would return from vacations or weekend trips and share testimonies that went something like this: "While we were gone, it was so good to visit a church where exciting things are happening for Christ. We know things like that cannot happen in a church like ours, but it is wonderful to see them happening somewhere." They viewed themselves as support staff for those who were on the front lines promoting the gospel of Christ, instead of recognizing the potential for ministry right here at home.

Statistics for the LaMoure Church of the Nazarene showed a steady decline over the past several years. Between 1983 and 1988, membership had declined four out of five years, with a high of 50 and a low of 37. Sunday School attendance had declined four out of five years, with a high of 55 and a low of 37. Morning worship attendance had declined for seven straight years—1981 through 1988—with a high of 65 and a low of 46. Since 1988 an additional 40 percent of the congregation has been lost through natural attrition.

Much of the reason for this steady decline can be traced to statistics that showed a declining community with a closed door for the gospel. LaMoure County showed a decrease of 12 percent in population from 1980 through 1988, with just over 7 percent of this decrease occurring from 1984 through 1988.

According to *Churches and Church Membership in the United States,* LaMoure County reported church adherents in excess of population![3] Possible explanations for the discrepancy included a census undercount, church membership overcount, or a difference in county of residence from the county of church membership. According to Rich Houseal, church growth research consultant for the Church of the Nazarene in Kansas City, "What this means in practical terms for the LaMoure Church of the Nazarene is that any growth would actually come from those who are affiliated with other churches, and not so much from individuals unaffiliated with any church."

When all of the available data is collected—the opinions of church growth experts, the statements of people who are familiar with this church, and church and community statistics—there seem to be more than enough reasons to forget growth and merely try to survive.

On the contrary, the church in LaMoure has become a place where exciting things are happening for the cause of Christ. A church that averaged 46 in morning worship in 1987-88 did not have a Sunday under 50 in morning worship in 1989-90. The church is now ministering to 25 new families through its various ministries. Forty every-Sunday attenders are new to the church. On any given Sunday, over 50 percent of the congregation are those who were not here five years ago. The church is currently ministering to approximately 125 people weekly in various ways. This amounts to over 10 percent of the population of LaMoure. The steady decline has been turned around.

A Look at the Statistical Progress

	1987-88	1988-89	1989-90	1990-91	1991-92
Church Membership	37	43	45	45	47
New Members	2	7	6	0	3
New Nazarenes	1	5	6	0	1
Morning Worship	46	61	65	68	72
Sunday School	38	56	77	90	97
Responsibility List	94	158	171	188	198
Sunday Evening	25	35	38	42	45
Raised for All Purposes	$44,600	$51,644	$55,691	$64,330	$76,491
Church Indebtedness	48,971	39,455	31,843	19,340	-0-

	Total No. Growth 1987-92	Total % Growth 1987-92
Church Membership	10	27%
New Members	18	38%
New Nazarenes	13	27%
Morning Worship	26	56%
Sunday School	59	155%
Responsibility List	104	111%

Sunday Evening	20	80%
Raised for All Purposes	$31,891	72%
Church Indebtedness	-0-	100%

10% Mission Giving

1987-88	$4,367
1991-92	$7,015

Statistics, though important, tell just a part of the story. Behind the statistics are people. Each number represents a person, and it is he or she who really matters to the church. As someone has put it, "We count people because people count."

This church is excited by what God is doing in its midst. The Church of the Nazarene has become the talk of many in the community. People call it "the church that loves people . . . the church that gives of itself to its community."

C. Peter Wagner has said the following.

> Church growth has four dimensions. In commending the church at Jerusalem, chapter two of Acts says that the church is to grow up in our personal and corporate spiritual life; the church at Jerusalem matured in its understanding of apostolic teaching by gathering together for the breaking of the bread, prayer, and fellowship. Second, they grew together. In fact, the Jerusalem church lived together in a community; they weren't "lone-ranger" Christians. Third, they grew out. They did not exist for themselves; they reached out into the community and performed works of charity, which in turn created a favorable impression of the church in its neighbors' minds. And fourth, they grew in numbers. As a result of the way those people lived, the Lord added daily to the church such as should be saved. A church that is pleasing God grows in these four ways.[4]

The LaMoure Church of the Nazarene is now a growing church as defined above by Dr. Wagner. Praise God for all the things He is doing in our midst!

It can happen in the small-town church! I am not a "superstar" pastor who possesses a Midas touch. Rev.

Plemons believed this church could provide a time of healing for my ministry. I left a pastorate some five months earlier, believing I had missed God's calling. I was willing to do whatever He willed—except pastor another church! I had pastored three churches, and to all appearances I had failed. Yet, I was God's man for this church. Although I may very well pastor the best group of people in the Church at large, the record will show that they were a church on the decline, facing some very difficult days. God's plan was for pastor and people to unite under the Holy Spirit's direction and anointing and revitalize the LaMoure Church of the Nazarene.

LaMoure should be an *example* of what God can do in the small-town church and not an *exception*. What God has done here He can do anywhere as His people are obedient to His will.

* * *

An Exercise Toward Revitalization

1. On a scale of 1-5, evaluate your church's current growth in its four dimensions:

    Growing up
    Growing together
    Growing out
    Growing numerically

    If your combined score is 19-20, your church is on target. If it is 14-18, your church is moving in the right direction. If the score is 9-13, your church is showing some sign of growth. If it is 8 or below, you have a big job ahead of you; but with God's help, it can be done!

2. List examples of your church's growth in each of these four areas:

    Growing up
    Growing together

3. Claiming the promises of God's Word, list five reasons why you believe God will revitalize your small-town church.

2

The Role of Revival in Revitalizing the Small-town Church

If my people, which are called by my name, shall humble themselves, and pray, and seek my face, and turn from their wicked ways; then will I hear from heaven, and will forgive their sin, and will heal their land.

2 Chron. 7:14

The revival we speak of here is not a series of special services nor an appeal to sinners. Revival is the need of God's people, the Christian believers. Revival is a fresh outpouring of God upon His Church.

Revival is needed! Without a genuine revival, the small-town church will never be revitalized. The Psalmist prayed, "Revive us again" (85:6). Revival is not a once-for-all-times occurrence. Habakkuk prayed for God to revive His people "in the midst of the years" (3:2).

Revival is beautifully illustrated in nature. Following winter's dormancy, the earth bursts forth with new life in the spring. God's people, individually and corporately, also need revival to overcome seasons of dormancy and to burst forth with new life. Revival can bring new life to an old church. God can revive the small-town church of today. Revival can end laxness, stagnation, hypocrisy, selfishness, materialism, criticism, loss of energy, and staleness. The reviving touch of God is an essential part of revitalizing the small-town church.

THE STEPS TO REVIVAL

1. Humility is essential.

God is the only source of revival, and He gives revival only to those with humble spirits and contrite hearts. We will be the recipients of real revival only if we mean business. Our gimmicks and games will not impress God. Revival will come to the small-town church only if its people are ready to die to themselves and depend upon Him as their only hope and first source of help. We have to be willing to do whatever God requires of us to experience genuine Spirit-sent revival.

2. Prayer is indispensable.

The power of prayer unleashes the reviving work of God upon His Church. A church will never be any stronger than its prayer life. Prayer is the lifeline that connects Jesus and His Church. Prayer is the key to the Christian life. What would your marriage be like if you did not talk to your spouse any more than you talk to Jesus? Prayer is as essential to Christian experience as oxygen is to human existence. James 5:16 says, "The effectual fervent prayer of a righteous man availeth much." This means that when we pray, we should come before God with a clear conscience and a clean heart—and expect results.

3. Desire must prompt us to seek God.

If we want God's presence in us and approval of us, we shall receive them. Jesus said, "Seek, and ye shall find" (Matt. 7:7; Luke 11:9). We need to seek God in His sanctuary, for He will be found as we worship Him. We need to seek Him in the fellowship of two or three gathered in His name, for there He will be "in the midst of them" (Matt. 18:20). We need to seek Him in His Word, for it declares Him. We need to seek Him in His creation, for it speaks of Him. We need to seek Him through service, for what is done for others is done for Him. We need to seek Him in the stillness, for the Psalmist said, "Be still, and know that I am God" (46:10). If we will truly seek God, we will really find Him.

4. Revival will not come without repentance.

Before we can be revitalized, we must first be revived. God calls His people to turn from their wicked ways. Does all we think, say, and do bring honor and glory to the name of Jesus? Are there things in the life of our church that are a disgrace to the cause of Christ? Repentance is for Christians as well as sinners, for the church as well as the individual believer. Repentance is an admission of being less than what God wants us to be, and a resolution to live up to God's expectation for us.

GOD'S REVIVING WORK

1. God hears us when we pray.

When we have met the conditions for revival, we receive special attention from God. Revival clears the channel through which His blessings flow to us.

2. God forgives us when we repent.

Whenever God corrects, He gives direction. Whenever He convicts, He gives hope. Whenever He exposes our guilt, He shows us the way to forgiveness. God offers forgiveness to the believer and to the church. Not only does God forgive, but also He forgets. He does not hold grudges. Many churches need to put the past behind them, let it be covered in the sea of God's forgetfulness, and move on to become all He wants them to be.

3. God heals broken relationships.

God can and will heal the hurts of the small-town church. It is time to move past what used to be and what should have been to what we can become with God's help.

Unless we find healing, our hurts will hinder us from becoming the revitalized small-town church. There is healing in Jesus for the church that will receive it. God desires to unite the church in fellowship and mission.

THE RESULTS OF REVIVAL

When individuals are revived, the church is revived. When God's Church is revived, it operates at maximum efficiency. A church right with God is a church on the move. When our relationship with God is what it should be, we will find ourselves in the process of being revitalized.

1. When revival fires are burning, one is enabled to love everybody. He loves God with all his heart and wishes he could love Him more. He loves others as Jesus loves him, and he is willing to give himself sacrificially for them.

2. Complacency dies when revival comes, for revival gives the church a new vision of its potential. Jesus will give the church a vision of what it can be. He can give us a vision of our mission. When revival comes, Jesus gives us an urgent burden for the lost.

3. Revival puts cheer into the giving of our treasures, time, talents, energy, and selves, and "God loves a cheerful giver" (2 Cor. 9:7, NKJV). God can use any gift, but there are some He can use better than others. The difference is not the value of the gift but the generosity and attitude of the giver.

* * *

An Exercise Toward Revitalization

1. Open yourself up to a penetrating search of the Holy Spirit into your life and the life of the church. Ask Him to show you any need for revival in your midst.

2. Write out a personal prayer for revival in your life and in your church.

3

Rekindling the Flame in the Small-town Church

Behold, all ye that kindle a fire, that compass yourselves about with sparks: walk in the light of your fire, and in the sparks that ye have kindled.

Isa. 50:11

Revitalizing the small-town church never happens instantaneously, but it comes about as the result of a working process. Hot coals smoldering in a fire ring will never kindle into flame unless built upon and worked with. The smoldering church will never rekindle its flame until it undergoes a similar process. That which separates smoldering coals from roaring flames is much like that which separates potential from reality in the life of a church.

My dad is a master fire builder, because he would rather work with a fire than watch one. If we are to be successful in revitalizing the small-town church, we must be more interested in working than watching.

1. Start with the hot coals; work with what you have.

We often view our church situation and begin to make excuses for not being the church we think we should be or wish we were. Depending upon our local situations, we may think and say things like the following: "If only we had a piano player; if only we had more money; if only we had more resources; if only we had better facilities; if only we had more workers; if only we were bigger; if only . . . then we could be the church we should be." I wonder if there are any small-town churches that have not said at some time, "If only we had a piano player, then we could be the church we should be." If that is true, some churches could never amount to anything, for they do not even allow musical instruments in the church. I am not suggesting that a church should ignore its limitations, for each church has them, whether admitted or not. Rather, a church needs to understand what its limitations are. It needs to face up to them, but it does not have to dwell on them.

Instead of dwelling on the "if onlys," a church needs to emphasize the "with onlys" of its situation. We need to realize that every situation has its plusses. No matter how bad things might be at his church, one must believe it has some good things going for it. He must identify them and begin to build upon them. The plusses in a church's situation are its hot coals. As a church builds upon them, it can move toward the rekindling of its flame.

2. Add the kindling of planning, structure, and organization.

"Those who aim at nothing will hit it every time." That saying surely applies to the work of the church. The reason many have never accomplished much for the cause of Christ is that they have failed to lay before themselves distinguishable goals. When one does not know where he is going, he will not know when he gets there. It is not enough to be busy for the sake of Christ. Our activities must have a reason. If a congregation would revitalize its small-town church, they must organize for success. The church can function properly only within a structured system, and thus avoid chaos and anarchy. Actions are most advantageous when they fit into a plan. The church cannot operate on whims or emotions. Kindling will never produce a roaring flame, but it will produce a spark, whereas logs would smother the coals. Planning, structure, and organization will never in themselves revitalize the church, but they can add a spark to the process.

3. Fan the flame; use programs.

Life can also be added to a fire with a breath of fresh air. A fire about to be smothered out can be revitalized by fanning the flame. In the church, new or refurbished programs can serve to fan the flame, adding fresh air and new hope to the life of the church.

Programs must never be viewed as ends in themselves, but always as means to some higher end. Good programs are not our goal, but they will help us accomplish our goals. Good programs are never our purpose, but they will help us fulfill our purposes. Good programs are not the ministry of our church, but they will enhance and advance our ministry. We must always remember that programs are designed for people, not people for programs. If the program is the focal point of the church, the church needs a spiritual overhaul.

4. Add the logs: people.

It is the burning of logs that produces a long-lasting, roaring flame. The logs of the Church are people. The Church Jesus is building is a living organism. We are the building of Christ, living stones. A song written by Richard Avery and Donald Marsh, often sung by the children of our churches, beautifully describes this concept. It says, "The Church is not a building, / The Church is not a steeple, / The Church is not a resting place; / The Church is a people. / I am the Church, you are the Church, / We are the Church together! / All who follow Jesus, all around the world; / Yes, we're the Church together!"*

Churches have survived, at least for a time, without facilities, programs, finances, and preachers; but a church

---

24

is not a church without people. Therefore, if the church is to be the church, it must be *for* people. Let us never get to the place where we become so wrapped up in planning, structure, organization, and programs that we lose sight of the people. The following statement has been adapted from one commonly seen in various business establishments to refer to the local church and its relationship with people.

People are

. . . the most important element of the church. Without people, there would be no need for the church.

. . . not cold statistics, but flesh and blood—human beings with feelings and emotions like our own.

. . . not individuals to be tolerated so we can do our thing—they *are* our thing.

. . . not an interruption of our work, but the purpose of it.

. . . doing us a favor by giving us an opportunity to serve them. We are not doing them a favor by doing so.

Priority given to people affects the way both pastor and laypersons view their ministry.

5. Add the fuel: the anointing of the Holy Spirit.

Nothing produces a roaring flame more quickly than a cup of fuel. The Holy Spirit is the Fuel of the Church. His presence and power sets the Church apart from all other organizations and institutions. The anointing of the Holy Spirit is the beauty and the moving force of the Church. The Church is bankrupt without God the Holy Spirit. Only one thing is absolutely essential as a congregation gathers to worship God—the presence of the Holy Spirit in their midst. Worship and service without Him would be a waste of time. Without Him we might as well close up, padlock the doors, and put the property up for sale.

The church ceases to be the church when it ceases to be God's. It is God who gives the increase; it is Jesus who builds the church; and it is the Holy Spirit who is present when even two or three gather together in Jesus' name. Remember, nothing produces a roaring flame better than a cup of fuel, but to sustain the flame requires something to ignite. Can the Holy Spirit set us on fire for the cause of Christ and His Church?

6. Avoid dousing with water: "Quench not the Spirit."

Writing to the Thessalonians, the apostle Paul said, "Quench not the Spirit" (1 Thess. 5:19). As a boy, I remember going camping with my family. The highlight of every day was sitting around the campfire at night. When it was time to go to bed, we would pour buckets of water over the fire until it was out; no flame, no hot coals, nothing left. Nothing will kill a beautiful fire like great amounts of water. We must beware lest we douse the fires of revival in the church.

Before squelching the plans of people, one must consider that they may be following the mandate of God. When Nehemiah arrived in Jerusalem, he faced much opposition and many obstacles in building the wall. His foes felt they were squelching the plans of man when in reality they were obstructing the mandate of God. Let us be cautious lest we, like they, end up fighting against God. Problems will always be present in the church.

When I was a teenager, my pastor told me that if I ever found the perfect church, I should not go there, for it would cease to be perfect upon my arrival. Our human imperfections will lead to problems in the church. However, with God's help, as much as is possible, one should always be a part of the solution and not a part of the problem. We want to help the cause of Christ and never harm it.

May the following statements serve as our standard as we seek to live for God and keep revival fires burning: Do not stand in the way of God. Do not oppose the will of God. Do not amend the plan of God.

* * *

An Exercise Toward Revitalization

1. List the good things (plusses) about your church's present situation.

2. Ask God to show you any way in which you have stood in the way of God, refused the will of God, or amended the plan of God. If He shows you anything, repent of your fault and move forward toward the revitalization of your church.

3. Identify the "if onlys" of your situation, turn them over to God, and emphasize your plusses.

4

Developing the Microchurch for the Microcommunity

Now unto him that is able to do exceeding abundantly above all that we ask or think, according to the power that worketh in us, unto him be glory in the church by Christ Jesus throughout all ages, world without end. Amen.

Eph. 3:20-21

Many homes have two ovens—a conventional oven and a microwave. They do many of the same things, but they do them differently. Such is the case with the church in the large metropolitan area and the small-town church. Each community is different, but the results should be the same in ministering to the people of these communities.

AN UNDERSTANDING OF TERMS

In the interest of presenting the concept of developing the microchurch for the microcommunity, let us look at definitions for some of the terms that will be used.

The microcommunity is the independent small town with a population of 15,000 or less that is capable of providing its residents with all of their essential needs and services.

The microchurch is the church located in a microcommunity that is able to provide for its parishioners all their spiritual and other related needs.

The megacommunity is an urban area with a population of more than 15,000. Megacommunity is a reference to the large people centers of the world, to the masses of humanity that congregate within its broad borders.

The megachurch is the church located in a megacommunity. It is a church with tremendous potential. It is a church with a mass of humanity right outside its door. It is a church with thousands within its reach.

A CHURCH FOR A COMMUNITY

In discussing foreign missions, much is said about adapting the Christian Church and its ministry to the culture of the foreign community without diluting the message. The same approach must be taken by the church in the United States and Canada. There are vast differences between a community with more than a million people and a community of 1,000 people. Chicago and LaMoure, N.Dak., are less than 1,000 miles apart geographically, but culturally they are a world apart. They are as different as night and day. A church taken out of Chicago and placed in LaMoure would be like a fish out of water, without chance of survival. Likewise, a church taken out of LaMoure and placed in Chicago would not survive. It would be swallowed up almost immediately.

It is essential that churches fit into the communities they call home. The apostle Paul said, "I am made all things to all men, that I might by all means save some" (1 Cor. 9:22). He was a man who adapted to each situation in order to bring honor and glory to Christ. In much the same way, each church must adapt to the community in which it is placed, so bringing honor and glory to Christ.

The Megachurch for the Megacommunity

We hear much today about the megacommunity and the megachurch. We are part of a society that markets the masses. Businesses are geared toward reaching areas where the most people are. Why reach 1 person when you can reach 100 people?

The thrust of the church today is to the megacommunity. Many denominations have accelerated their efforts to the megacommunities in recent years. The Church of the Nazarene launched their Thrust to the Cities ministry in the mid-1980s. Thrust cities include Chicago (1986), Mexico City (1987), New York and Los Angeles (1988), Paris and São Paulo (1989), Toronto (1990), Seoul (1991), San Francisco (1992), Calcutta and Berlin (1993), Moscow (1994), and Nairobi and Houston (1995). These thrusts are necessary and positive. I believe in the ministry of our denomination to the megacommunity. It is a vital part of our mission and deserves all the attention it gets.

In 1989 my family and I visited one of our megachurches. There were more people in that church on an August morning than there are residents in LaMoure. I would never want to underestimate the value of that church's ministry, which touches the lives of thousands of people through its worship services. Another megachurch we visited on that same vacation centered its ministry around missions and reaching the needs of the total man. In the month before our visit, this church had provided for the needs of over 3,000 people by supplying food, clothing, furniture, rehabilitation groups, transportation, shelter, counseling, and church services to these people. The ministry of the megachurch is vital.

There is plenty of room in this world for megacommunities and microcommunities. As long as both communities exist, there will be a need for megachurches and microchurches. However, emphasis upon the mega-church should not result in the neglect or detriment of the microchurch. Someone once said to me, "Why are you wasting your time in a place like that? Recently I preached in a church of thousands. The church you are serving could never be that big, even if you reached every resident of your community."

In the push toward the masses, let us never forget the significance of one. Every small town across our land has people who need Jesus. Whether in the ministry of the megachurches or the microchurches, may we always be about the business of reaching people for the Kingdom.

THE MICROCHURCH FOR THE MICROCOMMUNITY

It is vital that the microchurch find its niche both in our denomination and in our communities. The micro-church is vital to the denomination of which it is a part. Approximately 50 percent of all Churches of the Nazarene in the United States and Canada are found in microcom-munities, defined as non-urban-area communities of less than 15,000 population. On the Dakota District, 30 church-es—nearly two-thirds of the total churches on the dis-trict—fit into this category. The church I pastor is an ex-ample of a microchurch located in a community of 1,000.

Total Churches of the Nazarene in the United States
and Canada 5,057
Churches of the Nazarene in communities with less than
15,000 population, outside urban areas 2,489
(49.2%)
Churches of the Nazarene in communities with greater
than 15,000 population, outside urban areas...........366
(7.2%)
Churches of the Nazarene in communities with less than
15,000 population, in urban areas............................631
(12.5%)
Churches of the Nazarene in communities with
greater than 15,000 population, in urban areas....1,571
(31.1%)[1]

The small-town church is also a vital part of the small town in which it is located. It adds to its community atmosphere, attitude, and appearance.

As long as there are small towns, they will need churches. Small-town churches today must be revitalized, that they may fulfill their purpose in the denomination and their communities.

Many things are working in the megachurch that would not work in the microchurch. However, many things are working in the megachurch that can either be used as they are or adapted to the microchurch situation. The microchurch is not a miniature form of the megachurch. It has a nature and characteristic all its own. The microchurch should never be viewed as a second-rate church. Its potential is at least as large as the community in which it is situated. In many cases, the microchurch could become *the* church of its community. The opportunities awaiting the microchurch are as vast as the promises of God.

A microwave can be used for many wonderful things. Many exquisite dishes and delectable treats may be prepared in a microwave. Yet the microwave is at the mercy of the individual who masters its controls. Although I have been told of the enormous potential of a microwave, I use it almost exclusively for heating up leftovers. Someone once told me that I was wasting a wonderful machine on such a limited task.

God has much that He wants to do in our microchurches if we will allow Him to take over the controls and if we will follow His direction. God has mighty plans for the microchurch if the pastors and people of these churches will be all that God wants us to be.

* * *

An Exercise Toward Revitalization

1. List what your church has done to adapt to your community in ways that bring honor and glory to Christ.

2. List what your church needs to do to adapt to your community in ways that bring honor and glory to Christ.

5

The Miracle of Church Growth

But Jesus beheld them, and said unto them, With men this is impossible; but with God all things are possible.

Matt. 19:26

Mark 2:1-12 records the healing of a man with palsy. Miracles are the work of God, but God often uses human assistance to accomplish His miracles, as this Gospel story shows. Some parallels can be drawn between this miracle of healing and the miracle of church growth.

THE NEED

In scanning the Gospels, we find, with few possible exceptions, a common component in all the recorded miracles of Jesus: each one met a need. Jesus did not flaunt His power. Upon analysis, the miracles of Jesus disclose two purposes—they met needs and they brought honor and glory to God.

In this case, the palsied man provides the need. His need is twofold—physical and spiritual. He suffered from a paralysis that left him totally dependent upon others. This physical need was obvious to all who saw him. His spiritual need was discerned by Jesus, who knows the inner lives of persons. Only a miracle could meet the need of restored health and eternal life.

The small-town church is also in need of the miraculous. Like the man with the palsy, the need may very well be twofold. First, there is the external need, obvious to simple observation. A church steadily declining year after year has a need. A church whose facilities and grounds are unkempt has a need. A church whose services lack the presence and anointing of the Holy Spirit has a need. However, this may be only a part of the problem. The church may also have an interior need, a need that cannot be seen with the human eye. A church without a proper self-esteem has such a need. A church with a divisive spirit has a spiritual problem. If we are to see miracles happen in the lives of small-town churches, we must be willing to recognize the need and then bring it to Jesus.

The Divine—Jesus

A miracle is divine intervention within the human realm. A miracle occurs when God enters the scene and moves with power and glory. Miracles are the work of Jesus. People can do some wonderful things, but only Jesus can do the miraculous.

Jesus is the Great Physician. He made the man with the palsy whole. He brought sight to the blind, hearing to the deaf, strength to the lame, health to the leper, freedom from oppression to the demon-possessed, and life to the dead. He can also bring healing to His Body, the Church.

Jesus is the great Church Builder. In Matt. 16:18 He said, "I will build my church." Sometimes we misunderstand our place in the building of His Church. He is the Architect and General Contractor; we are to be His tools. We are not in charge; we are His charges. God does not call us to success, but to faithfulness. Results are in His hands, but willingness is in our hands. Jesus will do miracles for the small-town church as His people are obedient to His will.

THE CARRIERS

Unique to this miracle are the four men who carried the man with the palsy to Jesus. They bridged the gap between what was and what could be. They were the link between the need and the divine.

Whether the initiative was theirs or was exercised by the paralytic, we are not told. We do know that their willingness made this miracle possible. What if even one of these men had refused to assist in this task? Would the others have given up also? Would they have decided to take their friend to Jesus anyway? Because of their increased load, would they have arrived too late, finding that Jesus had gone?

The miracle of church growth also requires people who will bridge the gap between present weakness and future strength. Who will carry the small-town church to Jesus? Pastor, will you help? God has called you to be His man for this position. Laypersons, will you help? God has not placed you in your church by accident. He has put you there to be a colaborer for the cause of Christ. Will you do your part? The district and the denomination represent the other two carriers. Their personnel, leadership, resources, and programs will assist you in carrying out the work of Christ. Will the absence of one carrier prevent a miracle from happening? Jesus will build His Church if His people will let Him.

THE COST

The four stretcher-bearers encountered a major obstacle when they reached the place where Jesus was preaching. How could they get through the multitude to Him? Unable to get through the door, they struggled up an outside stairway to the flat roof. They uncovered a section of the roof in order to lower the man to Jesus.

Whether the palsied man or those who carried him, someone was willing to pay the price to bring this man to the Miracle Worker. In tearing up the roof, they were saying, "We are willing to pay for the roof to be repaired, restored, or replaced, whichever is necessary."

The miracle of church growth will be costly to the small-town church. It may cost some wear and tear on the property, for a lived-in house always looks different from a showcase house. A growing church is a church full of activity and opportunity. This means programs that must be staffed and financed. It costs money to grow a church. It costs people something of themselves, for growth brings change. It may cost positions, for a growing church must make room for new leaders. It *will* cost something. Are we willing to pay the price?

THE RESPONSE

The scripture tells us that when the victim of palsy was healed, onlookers were amazed and praised God, saying, "We never saw anything like this!" (NKJV). That will be our response when God provides for us the miracle of church growth. We will say with the songwriter Fanny Crosby, "To God be the glory—great things He hath done." May we give unto Him the honor, glory, and praise due unto His name.

Certain others were critical of the miracle. They questioned, challenged, and doubted the works of Jesus. There are many who react in much the same way to the miracle of church growth. Over the last five years I have heard things like "Don't worry—you'll come back down to earth"; "I hope you will be OK when the bubble bursts"; and "This is surely good. I just hope it lasts." Even after God has worked a miracle, many people still choose not to believe He has. Their doubt must not be allowed to quench our faith.

* * *

An Exercise Toward Revitalization

1. Write down the price you are willing to pay personally and as a church to see your small-town church revitalized.

2. In all honesty, would your reaction to the revitalization of your small-town church be praise or criticism?

3. What are the needs of your church that should be brought to Jesus?

6

The Great Commission Then and Now

And he said unto them, Go ye into all the world, and preach the gospel to every creature.

Mark 16:15

THE GREAT COMMISSION—THEN

The Gospels tell us that before Jesus ascended into heaven, He gave His disciples a Great Commission to go into all the world. In the Book of Acts, He gives them directions for fulfilling that Great Commission: "But ye shall receive power, after that the Holy Ghost is come upon you: and ye shall be witnesses unto me both in Jerusalem, and in all Judaea, and in Samaria, and unto the uttermost part of the earth" (Acts 1:8). This is the key verse of the Book of Acts. This describes the process of world evangelization that was practiced in the first-century Church.

Theirs was a progressive ministry. Chapters 1—7 emphasize the evangelizing of Jerusalem. Chapter 8—12 emphasize the evangelizing of Judea and Samaria. Chapters 13—28 emphasize the evangelizing of the Gentile world.

Theirs was a Spirit-filled ministry. The first-century Church, empowered by the Holy Spirit, made a lasting impression on their world.

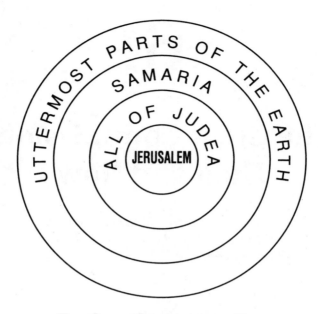

UTTERMOST PARTS OF THE EARTH

SAMARIA

ALL OF JUDEA

JERUSALEM

THE GREAT COMMISSION—NOW

Today the Church still finds a mandate for ministry in the Great Commission. Today's Church is called to "go . . . into all the world." But where shall we find our directions for fulfilling the Great Commission in our day? A modern-day paraphrase of Acts 1:8 might read, "But you shall receive power after the Holy Spirit has come upon you; and you shall be my witnesses to your responsibility list or extended church family, to your community, to your satellite communities, and to the whole world through your district and world missions." This describes the process of world evangelization that should be practiced in today's small-town church.

Too many small-town churches are ingrown and self-centered. If a church waits until it can afford to be an "others"-oriented church, it will never attain that status. There is no time like now to become a center for evangelization. We have an opportunity and an obligation to minister to our responsibility list or extended church family. This encompasses anyone who comes under the direct influence of our church.

We also have an opportunity to minister to the people of our community. The small-town church should make every effort to be a community church. We also have an opportunity to reach the people of our satellite communities. A satellite community is any community within 20 miles of our home community. Today's society is not hindered by distance. Many people will drive 20 miles or more to a church. An effort must be made to reach them. This expands the boundaries of ministry. We also have an opportunity to reach out through district and world missions. Our ministry in this area should include prayer, offerings, and, whenever possible, direct involvement and participation.

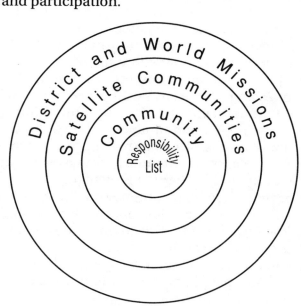

THE GREAT COMMISSION—FOR US

Each small-town church would find it helpful to apply Acts 1:8 to its local situation, for this scripture applies to our time and our place. A paraphrase of this verse, as applied to the LaMoure Church of the Nazarene, reads as follows: "But you shall receive power after the Holy Spirit has come upon you; and you shall be my witnesses to your responsibility list or extended church family in the community of LaMoure; to the satellite communities of Verona, Englevale, rural Litchville, Marion, Dickey, Grand Rapids, Berlin, Edgeley, Monango, and Fullerton; and to other small-town churches and district and world mission areas."

Uses of the responsibility list will be discussed extensively in Part II of this book. The ministry of the LaMoure Church of the Nazarene to its community will also be discussed extensively in Part II, but at this point I would like to talk about the community we serve—LaMoure, N.Dak. This community has a population of approximately 1,000. Target groups we focus on include those 55 years of age and above, which amounts to approximately 30 percent of our community. Those under 25 years of age account for nearly 40 percent of our community; and those between the ages of 25 and 34, the largest 10-year age-group in the adult population segment, make up approximately 10 percent of the population.[1] Knowing the composition of our community will assist us in reaching the people. The Church of the Nazarene is the only evangelical church in our community, and the harvest is plenteous.

We have nine satellite communities within 20 miles of LaMoure and two others just outside those boundaries. Many of the residents of these communities do business in LaMoure on a regular basis. None of these communities has an evangelical church. We could be their church. We already have people from several of these communities attending our church.

A church's mission to others must include direct and indirect missions. Indirect missions include informed, generous offerings and active prayer. Direct missions include teen trips, Work and Witness team members, and the sharing of what God is doing in our midst with other small-town churches.

THE GREAT COMMISSION—OUR MISSION

Our mission is the Great Commission, but let us not go about our mission unprepared. Scripture admonishes us to be witnesses *after* the Holy Spirit has come upon us and we have received power. A little done with God is better than a lot attempted without Him. We would not begin a long journey with an empty gas tank. We must not attempt God's work on an "empty tank." Through a Spirit-filled ministry, the small-town church can make a lasting impression on its world.

* * *

An Exercise Toward Revitalization

1. Write out a paraphrase of Acts 1:8 that applies to your local church's situation.

2. List the things that have been done in your church in the last year to fulfill the Great Commission.

3. List the things that have been done in your church in the last three years to fulfill the Great Commission.

7

Keep a Proper Outlook—
Emphasize the Positive

*I can do all things through Christ
which strengtheneth me.*

Phil. 4:13

WHAT DO YOU SEE?

An old adage says, "Life is what you make it." Everyone comes upon huge "boulders" that block the journey through life. How that boulder is viewed is all-important. One man will see it as a stepping-stone, while another man will see it as a stumbling block. Viewed as a stepping-stone, the boulder will be used to the traveler's advantage. As an obstacle to overcome, it represents an opportunity to triumph. Viewed as a stumbling block, the boulder will discourage the traveler. The obstacle will overcome him. He will give up and quit.

Every small-town church also faces boulders in its path. It cannot get around them. The boulder can represent so many different things—finances, facilities, personnel, programs, community receptivity, reputation, and attitude, to name just a few. However, by way of definition, a "boulder" is anything that comes between the church and God's intentions for it. The church can treat boulders in one of two ways: as stepping-stones or as stumbling blocks.

In every boulder God has provided a tremendous opportunity for victory. The church must not allow the devil to turn assured victory into abject defeat. We need to believe in God and His Church. A positive "we can" attitude should prevail in the church through the power of Christ. "Surrender" must be excised from our vocabulary.

A Proper Esteem

Many people never amount to anything in life because they believe they won't. Could this be the problem in many of our small-town churches? People or churches rarely exceed their expectations. If we set our expectations low, are we not limiting the potential of God? Can we begin to live according to the promises of God as they relate to the Church?

Numbers 13 describes the children of Israel as they encamped at Kadesh, just outside the Promised Land. Moses sent 12 spies into Canaan to scout it out and bring back a report. Let us lift from this story three would-be possessors of the Promised Land. Which one of these men would best represent your small-town church?

Talmai: A Man Who Thought Too Much of Himself

Talmai was one of the sons of Anak mentioned in the report of the spies. He was a giant. He possessed the land of Canaan by default. He received 40 extra years of life in the Promised Land because the children of Israel refused to take possession of God's promise to them. This is *not* how Talmai saw it. He thought he possessed the Promised Land on his own merit. He was a big man with a big reputation. He could take care of himself. He felt no need for assistance from God or man. He had everything under control until the children of Israel finally came into the Promised Land. In Hebron he was defeated by the invading Israelites.

The small-town church should never possess the spirit of Talmai. It is not who we are but *whose* we are that really matters. The church must never get "too big for its britches." We should never vainly "flex our muscles." We should never be the possessors of an overinflated ego, but rather have humility. The attitude of the small-town church should be that we need God more than He needs us. It is God who makes the church distinct. Without Him, the church would be just another social club or civic organization. Only with God can the church be what it is supposed to be.

Shaphat: A Man Who Thought Too Little of Himself

Shaphat, of the tribe of Simeon, the son of Hori, was one of the 12 spies sent by Moses to scout out the Promised Land. Their report, to which he consented, majored on the negative. The emphasis of their report was on the bigness of the problem and the littleness of themselves. They talked of the mighty soldiers, the walled cities, and the great giants they saw there. They saw themselves as grasshoppers in a land of giants, and that is what they became. They believed in the goodness of the Promised Land, but they never believed it could be theirs. They said, "We are not able . . . for they are stronger than we" (Num. 13:31, NKJV). They left God out of their plan, and 40 years later, when the children of Israel claimed possession of the Promised Land, God left them out of His plan. Only two spies—Caleb and Joshua—would be among the possessing forces.

The small-town church should never possess a spirit like Shaphat's. We must not allow ourselves to major on the negative. We can think and talk too much about what is wrong with us and not enough about what is right. Like Shaphat and his peers, who brought the negative report back to Kadesh, we will become what we think we are. If we see ourselves as grasshoppers, then grasshoppers is all we will be. The small-town church must believe that the promises of God are for them. Our small-town church can be a part of God's plan for building His kingdom if we trust Him.

CALEB: A MAN WHO THOUGHT OF HIMSELF AS HE SHOULD

Caleb, of the tribe of Judah, the son of Jephunneh, was one of two spies who brought back a positive report from their scouting trip to the Promised Land. The emphasis of their report was on God's promise and power. Their report did not ignore the negative aspects of the majority report; but it put them in their proper perspective: Yes, there are mighty soldiers, walled cities and giants, but they are not too much for our God. Yes, God promised us this land, and He has always kept His promises to His people. Yes, God has given this land into our hands; so what are we waiting for?

Caleb's attitude was "With God we can." He expressed his view to the people of Israel at Kadesh, but they did not share his faith. They rejected his report, and he was left to wander in the wilderness with them for 40 years. When they did enter the Promised Land, Caleb and Joshua were the only ones from their generation still living. Because they were faithful to God, He was faithful to them, and the Promised Land became their possession. Caleb never quit believing the promise of God.

The small-town church should have a spirit like Caleb's. Our emphasis should be positive in nature, based upon the bigness of God and the goodness of His promise. We cannot ignore the negative aspects of our situation. If we pretend there is not a negative side, we will only hurt ourselves. Instead, we must gain a proper perspective in regard to both the negative and the positive. We must understand that without God we do not stand a chance, but that *with* God we cannot miss. Pastor, laity, and God make an unbeatable team for the cause of Christ and the revitalization of the small-town church. With God we can!

If we fail to believe, we will also fail to achieve. The

loss of hope will drain all strength from our efforts. When we *know* we cannot, we *will* not. Belief fosters achievement. Increased hope accelerates our efforts. When we know we can, it follows that we will. With God's help we can see the small-town church revitalized.

* * *

An Exercise Toward Revitalization

1. Identify the "boulders" of your church's situation.

2. Identify ways in which you can turn your "boulders" into stepping-stones.

II

Implementing the Task

II

Implementing
the task

8

Define the Roles of the Pastor and Laity

And let the peace of God rule in your hearts, to the which also ye are called in one body; and be ye thankful. Let the word of Christ dwell in you richly in all wisdom; teaching and admonishing one another in psalms and hymns and spiritual songs, singing with grace in your hearts to the Lord. And whatsoever ye do in word or deed, do all in the name of the Lord Jesus, giving thanks to God and the Father by him.

Col. 3:15-17

Revitalizing the small-town church is a three-way partnership between God, the pastor, and the laity. Without the active and willing participation of all three, the church will never be revitalized. We need each other. In this chapter, we will consider the roles of the pastor and the laity in this process.

THE ROLE OF THE PASTOR

The pastor is called by God to his task. I did not choose to be a pastor; I was chosen. Rev. Robert O. Clark, my pastor during my formative teen years, once told me something like this: "If you can do anything with your life except be a preacher and can still be a happy Christian, by all means go for it. But if you cannot, then be the best preacher you can be, and be happy at it." He was himself a happy pastor, and his wise counsel has been very helpful to me.

The call to preach is still the high calling of God. It is crucial to the small-town church that their pastor has a clear calling to the ministry in general and to that church in particular. A pastor needs the assurance that his current assignment is a divine decree. I am in LaMoure, N.Dak., because God has put me here. I know I am God's man to pastor this people at this time.

I have never been a bivocational pastor, although many times I have wondered if I should be. This is a question faced by many small-town pastors. There are some situations that require a pastor to work secularly. I want to share some of the reasons I have never been a bivocational pastor.

First, I never had to be. Many times it seemed we could hardly seem to make ends meet, but somehow we have gotten by, for God has always provided.

Second, I did not have the time and energy to give to another job. It is doubtful our church would be experiencing the tremendous days we are having if I had been a bivocational pastor. I have often felt I needed the extra income of a second job, but I never felt I had the time to spare. There is no substitute for a hardworking pastor in revitalizing the small-town church, and I did not think I could work in the secular world and give the church the effort God deserves.

Third, I was afraid the church would become my second job. If I were a bivocational pastor, would my first loyalty be to the pastorate or to the secular job? Ideally, it would be to the pastorate, but practically it would probably be to the secular job. If the secular job were putting food on the table and checks in the mail, it could easily take precedence over the job that brought me to this community—God's call to pastor the church. Also, if there were a conflict between the two jobs, would I attend that preachers' seminar the church required of me or would I go to work at my secular job?

Fourth, I was afraid my secular job might hinder my willingness to follow God's call. What if God was leading me to another church? Would the financial provisions of the secular job make it hard or even impossible for me to accept the call?

These are some of the reasons I have never been a bivocational pastor. If you have to be one, and many do, my suggestions are simple: work at a secular job no more than you have to, and no longer than you have to. *Always* treat God's call to pastor as your first and most important job, and be the best pastor you can possibly be.

The pastor must be a man with a vision, a vision of what God has in store for this church. He needs to be like the prophets of the Old Testament who were energized to minister as a result of God-sent visions. He needs to see the big picture of what God has in mind for the church's future. He needs to be a possibility thinker, a man of great faith and a man with a positive attitude. He needs to be a man who sees tremendous potential in the midst of the present problems. Many small-town churches will soon perish without a vision of their God-given potential. The pastors of these churches must believe God can and will revitalize the small-town church.

The pastor must know where he is going. This is a vital part of his role in the small-town church. Once a vision has been caught, a plan must be developed to bring that vision to reality. In developing a plan, one may draw from his own creativity, the resourcefulness of fellow pastors, denominational programs and materials, and a vast supply of pertinent literature. To succeed, a plan will always require the support of administrative and organizational capabilities.

The pastor must be a man who leads others. Once a vision has been caught and a plan has been developed, implementation is necessary. Implementation requires a strong leader. A small-town church will go no farther than its pastor takes it. When I arrived in LaMoure, I caught a vision of what God could do in His church here, and plans have since been developed to translate vision into reality. In the implementation of those plans, the necessity of strong leadership has been realized.

A pastor should not expect more of his people than he expects of himself. He must lead by example. He should not expect his people to go on a wild-goose chase, but rather he must be able to transfer his vision from God to them.

His plans should not be dictatorially imposed upon his people. His plans must be amendable by them and owned by them and him together.

Leadership is often a lonely role, but the pastor cannot evade the burden. A church without a leader is not going anywhere.

The pastor must be a man of prayer. A prayerless pastor is not worth his weight in salt. He must be constantly in touch with God. His life should be saturated in prayer. The time, the place, the form, and the method of the pastor's prayer life should be of his own choosing. There are many good resources available to assist in the development of a meaningful prayer time.

A pastor must be cautious lest other worthwhile things crowd out his prayer time. He should never get so busy doing the work *of* God that he loses the time to be alone *with* God. Nothing pastors do is more important than the time they spend in prayer. Prayer keeps the pastor in touch with God, and without God there is no use attempting anything. Pastors, pray for your people, your mission field, and your own needs.

The pastor must be a man of the Word. He stands behind the pulpit to proclaim, not his message, but God's message. The message of God is rarely born on the Sunday morning of its delivery. It is born earlier in the heart of the messenger as a man of the Word. The pastor is called of God to ever-increasing familiarity with the Bible. As Paul urged Timothy, "Be diligent to present yourself approved to God, a worker who does not need to be ashamed, rightly dividing the word of truth" (2 Tim. 2:15, NKJV). "All Scripture is given by inspiration of God, and is profitable for doctrine, for reproof, for correction, for instruction in righteousness" (3:16, NKJV).

Every message should be saturated in prayer and anointed by the Holy Spirit. Pastors are called to be preachers. The pastor should never allow the proclamation of God's Word to take a backseat to anything.

The small-town pastor must be a man with a big heart. He must be a man who really loves people, *all* people, as God loves them. Love for God and for people created in His image must be at the center of everything a pastor is and everything he does. With God's help, a pastor must love every person who comes through the church's door. There is no substitute for a genuine love for people.

Such pastoral love must come to expression in compassionate service. The pastor's shoulder must be available for the weak to lean on and the hurting to cry on. He must truly be interested in them and be concerned with the things that concern them. He must both care *about* his people and care *for* them.

The pastor must be a man with a familiar face. Not enough can be said about the importance of a visible pastor in the small town. This matter will be addressed in chapter 12, but suffice it to say, this is an essential part of the pastor's role in the small-town church.

The pastor must wear many hats. In the day of the specialist, the small-town pastor must still be a general practitioner. His role includes many different things. Simply put, wherever he finds a need, he must try to meet it.

THE ROLE OF THE LAITY

1. A vital responsibility of laypersons is generous support of their pastor.

Pastoral support includes adequate financial remuneration. A small-town church needs a full-time pastor. This may not always be possible, but a congregation should do its best to free the pastor for maximum service by adequate financial support. God will bless the church that is generous to His servant.

Respect for the pastor as God's servant is crucial. It is possible for a minister to serve a church for years and never really be its pastor. It is possible to supply a pulpit, call on parishioners, carry out programs, and provide office management without ever really being a pastor. A pastor is more than a paid employee of the church who lives in the parsonage and occupies an office with the word "pastor" on the door.

There is much talk today about how a man must earn the position of pastor. Let us consider a differing opinion. I have truly been the pastor of the LaMoure Church of the Nazarene since the day I first accepted the call to come and serve this people. My people view the pastorate as a God-given call and not a man-given position. They truly accepted me as pastor of their church before I even arrived on the scene. In doing so, they were saying to me, "We will honor you as God's man for our church at this time; we will respect you as our pastor sent by God; we will follow you as God's leader for us; and we will heed your messages to us. We will do this until God calls you elsewhere or until you show us you are not worthy of your high calling from God to pastor us."

Their approach to the pastorate has made me a better pastor. It does not free me from being accountable to them, but it does constantly keep before me my accountability to God. Many men are out there just waiting for an opportunity to be truly a pastor to their people. Many small-town churches need to set their pastors free so that they can do the work God intends and the church needs. A church must allow the pastor to be truly its pastor.

The pastor's ministry should be undergirded with prayer. I regularly encourage my people to talk about me all they want, and I ask them to do it on their knees before Almighty God because I need all the help I can get. In over five years as their pastor, not a week has gone by that I have not heard some person in my congregation pray publicly for me, my family, and my ministry. It is not unusual for someone to stop me in the hallway at church or in the aisle at the grocery store, or to call me on the telephone, to let me know he or she has been praying for me.

It is hard to explain just how much the prayers of God's people mean to a pastor. A pastor friend of mine recently shared with me that he could count on one hand the number of times he has heard any of his people pray for him in the three years he has been their pastor. This is tragic! The prayer support of the laity is needed, for without God's help no pastor can make it.

Laypersons must participate heartily in the work of the church. As an avid sports fan, I understand how important a quarterback is to a football team, for he is at the center of the action. However, a good quarterback does not always make a good football team. It would be suicide to send a quarterback out onto the field by himself to face the 11 men of the opponents' defensive unit. The success of a football team depends upon the work of the 11 men who occupy the playing field at one time. It takes all 11 men giving their maximum effort to make a team the best it can possibly be. A mediocre quarterback could be the winning quarterback in the Super Bowl if he is at the center of an excellent football team.

The small-town church has much in common with a football team. The pastor is the quarterback. However, it is suicidal if the pastor is left to do everything that gets done. He cannot make it alone. Even a mediocre pastor surrounded by an active and excelling laity can be at the center of a revitalized church. It takes each of us doing his or her part to make the church what it should be. God needs the enthusiastic participation of the laity to revitalize the small-town church.

Earlier we affirmed that a church would never go any further than the pastor will take it. Now, speaking of the role of the laity, it may be said that a church will never go any further than the laity is willing to go. A pastor is a leader only if he has followers. Not every plan a pastor devises should be adopted, but when a pastor goes a whole year without one plan being adopted, he will cease to plan. The pastor can formulate excellent plans for ministry, but if the laity fail to work those plans, they will be good ideas that never got off the drawing board. A pastor can never be any more aggressive in leading than the laity are in following.

In Exodus 18, Jethro told Moses that it was not good for him to rule alone, for this was more than one man could handle. So Moses appointed leaders of 1,000s, 100s, 50s, and 10s. They handled the lesser things themselves and brought the more important things to Moses.

Likewise, it is not good for a pastor to lead alone, for this is more than one man can handle. Every church needs strong lay leaders to assist the pastor in the functioning of the church. God must always be the Boss of the church, but He needs strong leadership from both its pastor and its laity in carrying out the work He assigns the church.

2. Openness to change is another responsibility of the laity.

A small-town church in the process of being revitalized is also in the process of change. Openness to change is indispensable to church renewal. This includes changes in the church's program.

A recent change in this local church's program involves the Wednesday night format. We have moved away from the traditional Wednesday night prayer meeting and Bible study to a new and innovative ministry night. Each Wednesday service begins with a 30-minute intercessory prayer time, which is followed by an activity that either prepares us for ministry or involves us in ministry.

The first Wednesday of the month is a missions service. The second Wednesday is devoted to Christian training, with several workshops being run simultaneously. The third Wednesday is devoted to prayer fellowship groups. The fourth Wednesday is devoted to lay visitation, and the fifth Wednesday is a time for open discussion concerning the ministry of our church.

A revitalized church is a church with an increased level of activity to reach new people and meet the needs of its present people. We must be open to changes in constituency, extending a welcome to all people; to changes in leadership, incorporating new people into the leadership structure; and to changes in responsibility, with the understanding that revitalization demands increased responsibility. Where the laity is unwilling to change, it is unwilling to be renewed.

3. Faithful stewardship is a crucial responsibility of laypersons.

The faithful stewardship of the laity is essential to the revitalization of the small-town church. This would include the stewardship of their time, talent, and treasure. God expects us to be faithful to Him with all we have.

* * *

An Exercise Toward Revitalization

1. If everyone in your church were like you, what kind of church would yours be?

2. What do you perceive to be your role in revitalizing your small-town church? Be specific.

9

Examine Your Organizational Structure

Prove all things; hold fast that which is good.

1 Thess. 5:21

In Part I, we spoke of organizing for success and working within a structured system. A sound organizational structure will not guarantee success, but a faulty or absent one will almost always lead to failure. Organization is not glamorous, but it is essential. Proper organization is vital to the small-town church. I would like to share some of the key elements of our organizational system.

STATEMENT OF PURPOSE

Every church should have an agreed-upon statement of purpose, and it should be written down. We may all think we know the purpose of our church, but it is of little value to us until it becomes part of our organizational system. It should answer the questions "Why are we here?" and "What are we about?" It will establish a measuring stick by which we can evaluate the programs and ministry of our church.

Without an agreed-upon statement of purpose, we will never know whether we are fulfilling our purpose and getting done the job God has given the church. Without this statement, we will never be able to see how a program fits into our purpose.

The statement of purpose should be simple enough for all to understand it. It can be kept before the church family. We publish ours weekly in our church bulletin. A simple and short statement can be remembered by pastor and people alike. If a longer statement is necessary, a summarized version could be prepared for regular consumption.

Our Statement of Purpose
* To exalt God
* To encourage Christians
* To equip Christians for ministry
* To evangelize the world for Christ

STATEMENT OF POLICY

A statement of policy is our operator's manual. It defines the basic operations and procedures of church business. No church is too small to have one.

The original statement of policy can be drawn up by the pastor and board or by the pastor and a special committee of the board. Our policy statement is reviewed annually by a special committee and approved by the members at their annual meeting. This approval could be given by the church board, but membership approval provides increased involvement. Our policy allows for amendments or additions during the year by vote of the church board. In drawing up or reviewing the policy, one will want to consult the *Manual,* the District Finance Committee report, and, if possible, one or two other policy statements from neighboring churches.

A written and published statement will do many things. It will alleviate confusion regarding church policy. Questions of policy frequently arise in board meetings. Those who address the matter often have variant and conflicting understandings of policy. The church board secretary finds no record of former policy in the minutes. A published policy will eliminate such confusion and provide a point of reference for future questions of policy.

In addition, a published policy statement creates freedom for ministry for pastor and laity within established bounds. When working with a statement of policy, pastor and lay leaders alike need no longer feel as if they are walking through a minefield in doing their job.

Published policy statements also eliminate a multitude of special board meetings. Things that previously would require a special board meeting are now covered by the policy statement.

Areas that may need to be covered include church service times, special services, board meetings, board committees, church officers, hospitality committee, hospital remembrances, financial guidelines, Sunday School Ministries Board, pulpit supply and evangelism, pastoral care, special offerings, and general considerations. Each local situation may include other items that need to be covered.

ANNUAL OPERATING BUDGET

The small-town church is a big business, for it is God's business. Making money is not our business, but managing money is. The following areas should be covered in the annual operating budget: utilities, insurance, special assessments, district and denominational budgets, offering for educational institutions, building payments, pastoral care, maintenance and miscellaneous expenses, improvements, remembrances, office supplies, advertising, Sunday School, youth ministries, children's ministries, missions, and special services.

A good way to determine what should be included is to look at the expenditures for the last one year to three years. These figures will also help establish a budget, which should include columns for actual and projected figures for the year just completed, as well as columns for monthly and yearly projections for the coming year.

The annual operating budget should be drafted by the finance committee with the assistance of the pastor and be approved by the church board or annual meeting.

As a church, we are responsible for sound financial stewardship. Financial recordkeeping and financial planning are an essential part of that stewardship.

Another important matter is the ministry of finances. As a pastor, I offer no apologies for preaching and promoting storehouse tithing and giving to God of the firstfruits. God will take care of the church that takes care of His work. The money we put into missions and budgets is not thrown away but invested. None of us would ever decide not to pay the church's utilities, so how can we decide not to pay our fair share for the continuing of our church mission at large?

The annual operating budget will help us plan to meet all the financial responsibilities. One additional rule of thumb is not to budget for more money than was raised the previous year. Do not depend on an increase in annual income.

RESPONSIBILITY LIST

The responsibility list, which was formerly known as the Sunday School enrollment, is a valuable tool for ministry. As the name indicates, this list should consist of persons our church is responsible for ministering to. It is much more than an enrollment. Those we feel responsible for should include Sunday School regulars, Sunday School absentees, morning worship attenders, prospects, dropouts, weekday ministries enrollees, and any family members living in the same household. An expanded list should enlarge our ministry potential. This will happen only if we are serious about the list, treating it not as numbers to report, but as people to serve. We must *use* it. We publish our list annually and make revisions on an office copy throughout the year. The list is then promoted as a prayer and calling list.

ANNUAL REPORT BOOKLETS

These booklets are prepared for distribution at the annual meeting and throughout the year. They provide an accounting of the pastor and the lay leaders to the local church body. They also provide information about the church to its members and friends, serve as tools for our people's use (such as the responsibility list), and are an affirmation of what God is doing in our midst.

Included in our annual report booklet are reports, charts, membership roll, responsibility list, policy statement, and annual operating budget. We include in our booklet reports from the pastor, treasurer, church board secretary, NWMS president, Sunday School superintendent, NYI president, adult ministries director, children's ministries director, trustees, stewards, and hospitality and finance committees. They include the record and accomplishments of the previous year as well as plans for the year to come. They should always be optimistic and upbeat, emphasizing the positive.

Statistical charts accompany the goals established for the next year by the pastor and the church board. The charts range in length from those that cover the history of the church to those that are 10-year records, quarterly breakdowns, and monthly breakdowns with 3-year comparisons. They chart the record of the Sunday School, morning worship service, Sunday evening service, responsibility list, and the amount raised for all purposes.

CHURCH NOTEBOOK

We are compiling a church notebook to put all the information our families need to know about the church at their fingertips. These will be placed in three-ring binders so that if changes occur through the year, they can be inserted easily. They will have five color-coded sections. The first is a church directory, which lists each of our families, giving their names, addresses, and phone numbers. The second is a list of all our boards, committees, service organizations within the church, and any business relating to them. The third section is a church calendar for the year. The fourth is a list of all church schedules, such as those for ushers, greeters, nursery workers, providers of special music, etc. The fifth is for birthdays and anniversaries. The annual report booklet may be placed in the back of the notebook.

BOARDS, COUNCILS, COMMITTEES, AND OFFICERS

Positions of leadership are an important part of the church's organizational system. They are either mandated by the *Manual* or deemed necessary for the functioning of the local church. In accordance with the *Manual,* some positions must be filled by election, while other positions may be filled by election or appointment. It is important that positions are both filled and fulfilled and that councils, committees, and boards are both established and functioning.

The following offices are essential to every church: a church board and its committees, Sunday School Ministries Board, Missionary Council, and Youth Council. Sometimes it will be difficult for the small-town church to fill these groups, but wherever and whenever possible, it should be done. Other groups should be established when a local situation makes them necessary.

PRAYER MINISTRY

As mentioned in Part I, a church will never be any stronger than its prayer ministry. This ministry has been listed as a part of the church's organizational structure, for organization is essential in spiritual matters as well as in business matters. A spiritually organized church is a praying church.

Until recently in our local church, traditional Wednesday evening prayer meetings were held. These services included singing, testimonies, and Bible study, but prayer was our first priority. If all we got to on Wednesday night was prayer, we felt all right, because prayer is what we had come for. We now have a new Wednesday night format, which will expand our capacity for ministry. (This is addressed in the previous chapter.) Prayer still plays a vital role in this new format. The first 30 minutes of each Wednesday night's activity is spent in intercessory prayer, and the third Wednesday of every month is devoted to prayer fellowship groups.

In addition to the Wednesday night meetings, two groups meet weekly for special times of prayer. A women's prayer group meets Tuesday afternoons, and a men's prayer group Thursday mornings.

Special prayer emphases have included two 40-day periods of prayer and fasting. During these special times, at least one person from the church was committed to pray and fast at least one meal for each day of the emphasis. We recently conducted a similar emphasis of 365 days of prayer and fasting, which coincided with the Year of Prayer in the International Church of the Nazarene. Other special prayer emphases have included special cottage prayer meetings, Friday night prayer times at the church, and 10 Fridays of Prayer with 10 hours of consecutive prayer on 10 consecutive Fridays.

The regular prayer program of our church includes a Prayer Tree, which enables us to get a request to the people immediately via the telephone. The Prayer Tree differs from a prayer chain, which works by one person calling the person who follows him on a list, who in turn calls the next person on the list, and so on. We have found that when too many people are responsible for passing on information, the information has a way of getting changed along the way. Also, many times the chain is not completed.

The Prayer Tree works in the following manner. We

have one contact person, besides the pastor, whom people call with their prayer requests or praise reports. When a prayer need is called in to this person, he in turn calls three "branch" leaders, who each have a list of people they are responsible for calling. This method has proved to be very successful in getting accurate information to the church family in an efficient manner. There may be as many or as few branch leaders as are needed. However, the Prayer Tree works best if each person has no more than five or six families to contact.

A prayer request box in our foyer enables people to submit a request at any time, and our prayer request list is published weekly in our bulletin. This is in addition to our responsibility list, which also serves as a prayer request list throughout the year.

Prayer is the starting block for the small-town church. We will never get anywhere without it. At the same time, unless we put feet to our prayers and work together to see things accomplished, we will never see the checkered flag or become the revitalized small-town church.

* * *

An Exercise Toward Revitalization

1. Examine your church's organizational structure. Rate (0-4) each component of your church's organizational structure as follows:
   4—Very effective and beneficial
   3—Helpful and useful
   2—Adequate but could be improved upon and/or better used
   1—Inadequate or unused
   0—Totally ineffective or nonexistent

   Apply this rating to all components of your church's organizational structure:
   Statement of purpose
   Statement of policy

Annual operating budget
Annual report booklet
Responsibility list
Boards, councils, committees, officers
Prayer ministry

To evaluate your church's organizational structure, add the numbers from your ratings of the seven components.

25-28	Superior
20-24	Sturdy
14-19	Steady
10-13	Shaky
5-9	Sinking
0-4	Shambles

2. If your church does not have a statement of purpose, try writing one that answers the following questions:

    a. Why are we here?

    b. What are we about?

3. If your church has a statement of purpose, try using it as a measuring stick to evaluate your church's ministry and programs. Then ask yourself the following questions:

    a. Are we fulfilling our purpose?

    b. Are we getting done the job God has called us to do?

10

Develop a Plan

Trust in the Lord with all thine heart; and lean not unto thine own understanding. In all thy ways acknowledge him, and he shall direct thy paths.
Prov. 3:5-6

In Part I, the necessity of a plan was addressed. Now let us look at some practical suggestions for developing a plan for the small-town church.

GOALS

Goals serve as a target for the small-town church. They serve as a source of motivation toward the church's revitalization.

Three criteria should be met by any would-be goals. First, there must be a way to substantiate all goals. A goal is useful only if attainment can be verified. We need goals that can be used to measure our achievements. When we establish goals that cannot be measured, we will not know when they have been reached.

Second, goals should be challenging. A goal that fails to challenge us fails to fulfill its purpose. If we set goals in accordance with our abilities and resources, we are setting our sights too low. All our goals should require the assistance of God's presence and power. They should be more than we can do without Him. We should not be so realistic that no room is left for God to insert the seemingly impossible. In calculating our goals, we should consider our abilities plus our resources plus our God.

Third, goals should be reachable. If we set them too high, we may give up without trying. We must believe our goals are reachable before we will reach them. Reachable goals that are challenging will not limit God but will stretch us.

Goals should be established for Sunday School attendance, the number of new in-house Sunday School classes, extension classes, responsibility list, morning worship attendance, Sunday evening service, Wednesday evening ministries, new members, and total number of people ministered to weekly. In the area of finances, goals should be established for the following: monies raised for all purposes, mission giving, debt reduction, local outreach, and evangelism ministries.

Goals should also cover the scope of our ministry. They should be established for various time ranges. Short-range goals should include weekly standards, monthly standards, and annual goals. In setting annual goals, our church considered four viable options. The first was to turn the tide and reverse the downward trend. At the end of the 1987-88 church year, we showed an average of 38, a gain of 1 over the previous year's average. That was a significant accomplishment for us: a gain, a turning of the tide, the beginning of great things. The second option was to meet goals, which the denomination gives special recognition, such as a 5 percent attendance gain in Sunday School, 5 percent gain in worship attendance, 3 percent gain in membership, all budgets paid in full, 10 percent giving for missions, and, for our size of church, 6 new Nazarenes.

For many churches these would have been formidable goals. At that point, leading into the 1988-89 church year, we believed these would not challenge us enough, nor would they stretch our faith. The third option, which we accepted each of those first two years, was a 10 percent gain across the board. We have considered these goals to be both reachable and challenging. They have stretched our faith and demanded our energy. The fourth option was to equal or exceed the previous year's accomplishments. For us, that would have meant goals exceeding a 30 percent increase. Our decision was to accept 10 percent gains as our goal but to be open to whatever God wanted to do in our midst.

Once annual goals have been established, weekly and monthly standards should be set. Our weekly standard is the same as our annual goal. Our monthly standard has been to equal our annual goal and exceed the averages for the previous month and the same month last year. The weekly and monthly standards keep the annual goals before us all year.

Long-range planning is concerned with where the church will be in another 6 to 10 years. Long-range goals may emphasize the direction and focus of the church's ministry, but they should also give us some goals that can be substantiated. Within 10 years, it is our goal to be ministering effectively both in our community and to our satellite communities. Our desire is to do great things for God. Averaging a 10 percent gain per year over the next 10 years, we believe we can average between 100 and 150 in morning worship and minister to nearly 200 people in the course of a week. This has required expansion of our present facilities.

What will the future hold beyond the 10-year limit? We can envision a day when our church can run over 200 people in morning worship and minister to over 300 people weekly through our various ministries. We can also envision the possibility of establishing baby churches in some of our satellite communities. We believe in the God of the impossible.

Medium-range goals serve to form a bridge between short-range and long-range goals. They are concerned with where a church will be in the next two to five years. Our goals for this time period would include continued growth at a rate of 10 percent and the mobilization of the laity for ministry.

ANNUAL CHURCH THEME

The use of an annual church theme in the small-town church provides a focal point for ministry and helps us set objectives toward meeting our goals. It provides a rallying point in the church and gives us a tool with which to promote the ministry of the church during the year. During the last five years, we have used our theme in our weekly church bulletin and periodically in our worship services. We have promoted our themes with the use of cards, banners, bookmarks, flags, and related choruses.

To illustrate our use of the annual church theme, let us look at some information concerning our first two.

"The Time Is Now"—1988-89

"Sow to yourselves in righteousness, reap in mercy; break up your fallow ground: for it is time to seek the Lord, till he come and rain righteousness upon you" (Hos. 10:12).

This theme had five major objectives. First, we wanted to put an end to a pessimistic attitude that said, "It cannot happen here." Second, we wanted to put an end to a spirit of procrastination that said, "Maybe next year." Third, we wanted to put an end to the seven last words of a dying church: "We never did it that way before." Fourth, we wanted to generate increased activity in the church, believing it was essential to *do* something. Fifth, we wanted to generate enthusiasm, creating positive attitudes and a positive atmosphere in our small-town church.

I believe in the presentation of a theme and its objectives, but they are of little value unless the theme is used throughout the year. Two things that worked very well for us were the formation of many new ministries and the use of many special Sundays. (These will be discussed extensively in chapter 13.)

During our Wednesday night Bible study, we did a verse-by-verse study of the Book of Acts that took an entire year. It was good for us to study the work of the Holy Spirit in growing the New Testament Church while at the same time He was at work in the growing of our church.

Another problem we faced related to our ministries of finance. Four months into the 1988-89 church year there was great concern, for we had already fallen behind in the payments of our denominational responsibilities, or budgets, as they are more commonly known. Decisive action was needed, or we might be unable to meet these responsibilities for the first time in the history of the church.

The problem was overcome before *it* overcame *us.* We designated the last Sunday of September as "Miracle Sunday." All offerings received that day would go toward budgets unless otherwise designated. For this one Sunday, we led our people to give God what He deserved instead of what they could afford. For many of us, that meant giving God more than we made that week. We raised in that one Sunday $3,400, which was more than we were raising in a regular month at that time. This was a cash offering, not pledges! The next year we had our second Miracle Sunday and raised over $6,000 (actual cash offering). In 1990 the cash Miracle Offering was $7,400, and on this same Sunday in 1991, the actual cash offering was over $12,000! Praise God! We observe this Sunday early in the year so that we have several months left if we still owe on our budgets. When our offering has exceeded the amount needed to fulfill these obligations, we have designated the balance either toward our indebtedness or to enhance our local ministries.

Another thing we started that year was our teen mission trip. Our first trip, in the summer of 1988, took eight teenagers, my wife, and me to a "baby church" in the

Black Hills of South Dakota. While we were there, we conducted a backyard Vacation Bible School that ministered to approximately 60 kids. We also worked with the teens of the local church. This trip was financed primarily by our church.

The trip not only was good for the church to whom we ministered but also was of tremendous benefit to our teens and our local church. The following year, we again took a mission trip. The benefits are still being seen within our youth group and the church. These trips have been a time of genuine spiritual growth for our youth group.

These are just a few of the things we instituted during our emphasis "The Time Is Now."

"First Things First"—1989-90

"But seek ye first the kingdom of God, and his righteousness; and all these things shall be added unto you" (Matt. 6:33).

This theme had three major objectives. The first was to emphasize priorities. The second was to evaluate our priorities as a small-town church. The third was to increase the number of those involved in the ministry of the church.

One of the things we have done is to emphasize certain topics for a month at a time during our morning worship service. These topics have included prayer, stewardship, holiness, praise, children, and youth. Preaching each of these topics for one month increases the possibility of all my people hearing at least one message on each topic. These topics are priority items in the Christian walk and are especially helpful to new Christians and people who are new to the Church of the Nazarene.

Two surveys have been conducted as a part of this emphasis. The first was to evaluate the ministries of the church and consisted of three questions: (1) Which ministries of the church do you consider most valuable? (2) Which ministries of the church do you believe are unnecessary? and (3) Which ministries do you feel should be added to the church? Attached to the survey was a list of all the church's ministries. The result of this survey showed that the needs of our people were being met and that they were catching a vision of what God wants us to be.

The second survey was conducted in order to match individuals with areas of service within the church. Each person was given a list of service opportunities within the church, and they were asked to indicate where they were either willing or eager to serve. We are making every effort to expand our work force and better utilize our "people potential."

Planning Calendar

A planning calendar helps us do what we do for a reason. Each service, ministry, and activity of the church should fulfill our statement of purpose and accord with our stated objectives. A planning calendar enables the church to have a planned program. It should include all special emphases, special services, special offerings, special activities, regular services, and regular activities. When feasible, it should be the work of a planning committee. If this is not practical in a certain situation, it may have to be the work of the pastor until it becomes practical to have a planning committee.

The planning calendar should always be adopted by the local church board. The length of time covered in the plans is determined by the local church and its particular situation. A church that has never planned may want to begin a month at a time. To begin with, one may want to try either a three-month or four-month calendar, but not any longer. When the church has done it every three or four months for a year or more, it might be time to do it only once or twice a year. Whatever length of time chosen, one will find that it enables the church to run more efficiently and effectively.

* * *

An Exercise Toward Revitalization

1. Write out what you can envision God making of your church. Dream big.

2. Briefly sketch out goals, objectives, and programs necessary to make that dream a reality.

11

Get Ready for Company

*Let nothing be done through strife
or vainglory; but in lowliness of
mind let each esteem other better
than themselves. Look not every
man on his own things, but every
man also on the things of others.*

Phil. 2:3-4

WHY WOULD ANYONE CHOOSE OUR CHURCH?

Have you taken a look at your church from the outside
lately? This does not mean actually looking at your church
building from the outside, but rather looking at the
church from an outsider's point of view.

Many, if not most, who attend small-town churches
have been on the inside for a long time. Much too often
the church is run for those who, like ourselves, are on the
inside. We fail to take into account those on the outside
looking in. What does the outsider see when he looks at
our church? Why would anyone choose our church to be
his church home? Once he has come to our church, will
he ever come back?

All of this depends on us. If our attitude is, "What you
see is what you get; take it or leave it; it's good enough for
us; if it's good enough for you, come on in—if not, it's no

skin off our back," then they will probably never be back, and we will wonder why.

Have you ever found out that company was on the way to your home, and you tore through the house to make it look presentable? Let us consider some practical things that we can do to prepare for company in the church, for visitors can come when we least expect them, and we have only one chance to make a positive first impression.

Proper Facilities

We may be unable to do anything about the age or the size of our facilities. In many cases, like it or not, we have to live with what we have, at least for the time being. However, we must make the most of what we have.

Facilities and grounds should be clean and well kept. A church building may never be exquisite, but it can always be attractive. The grounds can be spruced up with flowers or shrubs or both. The walks should be kept clean and the grass mowed. The grounds should never be allowed to take on the look of the city dump, with a collection of discarded papers, cans, and bottles. Minor repairs to the facilities should be completed as soon as possible.

A gallon of paint can often do wonders for a room. A picture hanging in the right place or an up-to-date bulletin board can set off any classroom. In March 1989, the pastor who was here when our facilities were built returned with his family after a nine-year absence. He was amazed at the appearance of the building and stated, "It looks now like it did when we first moved in."

A church building must be functional, as well as attractive. A church must be in control of its building and never let the building have control over the church. The building must work for the members. The congregation should do whatever needs to be done to allow them to function at maximum efficiency and never let the limitations of the facilities limit their potential. When a congregation gets too big for their building, they must remodel, relocate, or start a baby church, but *never* quit advancing God's kingdom.

Our church is currently in the process of expansion. After two years of Sunday School classes meeting at the parsonage, we are now constructing a 40' x 60' addition to our present facility. This addition will enlarge our capacity for Sunday School, church fellowships, and children and youth ministries.

CONVENIENT PARKING

A church will rarely fit more on the inside than it can fit conveniently and comfortably on the outside. Poor parking can be a big problem. An off-street parking lot on the church site is ideal, but not always possible. If better parking than what is currently available can be provided, it should be arranged. If not, congregations should do the best they can but reserve the best parking places for visitors. Even if they go unused for months, these places should be left open for visitors, and all should pray for God's help in sending visitors to fill those spaces.

MEANINGFUL WORSHIP SERVICE

The following adages should apply to the worship service in the small-town church: "Something worth doing is worth doing right." "If you are going to have something, have something worth coming to."

We will rarely get more out of a service than what we put into it. All our services should be planned out, prepared for, and prayed for. We should never play the worship service by ear. We should bathe each service with prayer during the preceding week and anticipate God's best. We should plan the service and our part in it and be prepared to give God our very best.

I once talked to a woman who believed a pastor should stand behind the pulpit each Sunday morning totally unprepared and expect God to "zap" him with a sermon. Another woman once asked me if I preached only God-inspired messages or if I would ever consider preaching a series of sermons. The same God who is at work in the Sunday service can be at work in the preacher all week long. He who can lead a pastor to the right message for his people this week can lead him to the right messages for His people for the next month.

Pastor, there is hardly ever a good reason to go into any service unprepared. Holy Spirit-anointed preparation is vital. Every service should be a balance of structure and freedom. Rev. Clark, my former pastor, taught me never to walk onto the platform without a detailed schedule of service but always to be ready to discard that schedule without a moment's notice when the Holy Spirit directs, for God's presence is the most essential part of any worship experience.

Morning and evening services should be distinctive, significant, and equally billed. When the evening service becomes a second-rate service or a mere repeat of Sunday morning, it faces the possibility of extinction.

SPECIAL WORSHIP SERVICES

Every worship service should be special, but there should also be room in our schedule for special worship services.

Teen-Sponsored Service. The teens of the church are responsible for conducting the Sunday evening service. They lead the singing, share Scripture and poetry, receive the offering, lead in prayer, share a children's sermon, do puppets, and provide the music. Sometimes they will also take charge of the devotional. At other times they will turn that part of the service over to the pastor. In our church, the teens conduct a service every one to two months.

Ladies' Night. The women are responsible for conducting the entire evening service. Program and participants change from time to time, but these are always very inspirational services, which we have once or twice a year.

Laypersons' Night. Laypersons of the church take charge of the evening service. It is similar in format to the Ladies' Night service and occurs once or twice a year.

Singspirations. We all come together to share the musical talent of our own local church. We have from two to four of these services per year.

Revival Services. We have two revivals a year, one in the spring and one in the fall. We bring in an evangelist for these services, which run from Tuesday through Sunday.

Hanging of the Greens. This beautiful service, featuring the Chrismon Tree, is used to kick off the Christmas season in the church. It takes place the first Sunday evening of Advent and is conducted by candlelight until the end of the service, when the lights on the tree and Nativity set are lit. It is a truly meaningful service.

Advent. We incorporate a special segment into our morning worship service for the four Sundays before Christmas and then in our Christmas Eve Communion service. This features a devotional reading, a song, and the lighting of the Advent wreath in celebration of Christ's coming, both His realized nativity and His anticipated second coming.

Breadbreaking. We share in this special service one Sunday evening per year, usually in February. After the message, each person receives a small loaf of bread. The loaves represent each individual's life. As we go to each other, we offer others a piece of our loaves, symbolic of a part of ourselves, and share thanksgiving, appreciation, and love. It also provides an opportunity for the healing of damaged or broken relationships.

Communion. There is spiritual significance in religious rituals. While there are some who have lost the significance of the ritual in its practice, we can and should bring significance to the practice of the ritual. One way this can be done is through the use of variety in presentation. This is beautifully illustrated in our Communion services. In addition to the more traditional Lord's Supper service, we will have at least two very special Communion services each year.

Holy Week Communion is usually served on Maundy Thursday in the fellowship hall. Tables are set up in the form of a cross and covered with white paper or tablecloths. Candles are set on the tables and provide all the light that is necessary. At the head of the table sits a picture of Jesus and an empty chair, draped with a purple cloth, reserved for Him. A plate of unleavened bread and a cup of grape juice also sit at the head of the table.

The service consists of chorus singing, Scripture reading, special music, a devotional message, and the receiving of Communion. For this Communion, we share from the common loaf and common cup, although individual cups are available for those who prefer it that way. This is one of the most treasured services on the church's calendar. This past year when new round tables were donated for our fellowship hall, the board insisted on keeping enough of the old tables to have our Holy Week Communion Service.

Our Thanksgiving praise and Communion service is also held in the fellowship hall. The chairs are placed in an oval, with the Communion table at the top of the oval. It is a service of music, testimonies, a devotional message, and the sharing of Communion as a church family in the spirit of Thanksgiving.

A Waiting and Warm Welcome

Any visitor to our church should receive, within 30 seconds of his entrance, a friendly smile, a warm handshake, and a sincere welcome from a greeter standing at the door. That greeter should have a card or guest book on which to put the visitor's name and address. The greeter should also have a bulletin and a calendar or newsletter to leave with the visitor. The bulletin will enable him to feel more comfortable in the worship service and will, in addition to the calendar or newsletter, enable him to acquaint himself with the ministries of our church when he gets home.

Bulletins and calendars are a good ministry tool for regulars and visitors alike. They should provide information and look sharp so as to leave a favorable impression. They can be either Xeroxed or mimeographed on the church's own machines or on a borrowed or rented machine. Bulletin covers may vary. Covers in some church bulletins are made from regular copy paper, with a design sketched on the front. There is also the option of ordering bulletins from a place with dated bulletin covers.

Our bulletin covers are preprinted on heavy paper. They are set up to be folded in thirds. On one section is a sketch of our church. On the middle section is the church's address in the upper left-hand corner and space available for addressing and sending them to absentees, etc. On the other section is a list of our Articles of Faith and some informational statements about our denomination. There are many advantages to this type of bulletin cover. People who are looking for information about our church and what we believe can find it on the bulletin cover. Also, as few or as many bulletins as needed can be run off, and they will be uniform. There will always be enough bulletins for a growing congregation without having to constantly reorder.

An attempt should be made in the service to recognize visitors without embarrassing them. Every church should have a red carpet treatment policy. Every regular member of the church family should consider himself or herself a part of the greeting committee. No visitor should leave our church without having shaken dozens of hands and having received at least one invitation to dinner. Before the week is over, every visitor should have been contacted by the pastor and several laymen in one way or another. In most churches this will need to be organized, although in some churches people may prefer to do it on an informal basis.

A Genuine Welcome

We must extend a genuine welcome to anyone who comes through the doors of our church. We must be glad to see them and eager to keep them. Several years ago, I sat with a pastor friend in his study and chatted with an insurance salesman. The salesman, who was not acquainted with the work of our churches, asked, "What kind of people are you trying to reach?" He was stunned when our response was, "Any and every kind of people."

The small-town church must have an open door policy to anyone who comes. We must show an attitude of acceptance toward each person regardless of name, age, race, economic condition, social status, marital status, dress, denominational background, or life-style. This has been one of the successes of our church, reaching out to people who in some ways are unlike ourselves. This includes the person whose dress might be more appropriate in the gymnasium, on the beach, or in the dance hall; the person who entered the foyer of the church with the smell of alcohol on his breath or a pack of cigarettes in his pocket; a couple whose address is the same but whose last names are different. We might have condemned them and looked down our noses at them in rejection, but we did not. We loved them as Christ loves them, and they are becoming a part of us. We could have lost them, but instead we are winning them for Christ.

Every small-town church across the United States and Canada has unmarked reserved seats and parking places, whether we want to admit it or not. Observe the church you attend for the next four weeks and see if the greatest number of people don't sit and park in the same places week after week. We are creatures of habit, and that is OK as long as no harm is ever done. However, beware lest trouble strikes. A child says to his parent, "Mommy, someone is in our seat"; or a husband says to his wife, "I guess we are going to have to get here earlier next week if we are going to get our seat"; or a father says to his daughter, "You are going to have to get the lead out so that I can get my own parking place."

Maybe nothing was meant by any of these comments, but if they fall on the ears of visitors, it may cause discomfort and make their return highly unlikely. Let us give our seats and parking places away to visitors freely and graciously and treat every visitor as a Very Important Person.

A Prepared Welcome

Too often the church is unprepared for the essential "what ifs" of Christian ministry. We must begin now to develop ministries that will be needed in the revitalized small-town church. Sometimes if we wait until they are needed, it is too late. I would like to share one example of this from our personal experience.

Four years ago in our Sunday School we had no classes between the primary class and the teen class, because we had no children between those ages. But occasionally we would have fourth, fifth, or sixth graders visit in our Sunday School, and they would be placed in the primary class. They came only that one time! We decided at that point to establish a class, although at that time we had no children to fill it. A room and teacher were assigned, and material was provided. For many weeks that class had no one in it; then an occasional child or two came, and now we have four or five in that class every Sunday. They and their families amount to 19 people our church is ministering to. We could have lost the opportunity to minister to those families if we had not had an appropriate ministry for their children.

A Willingness to Move Beyond Single Cellness

Many, if not most, small-town churches are single-cell congregations. This means that, for the most part, everyone in the church is a part of everything that goes on in the life of that church. As a small-town church is revitalized, it will see an increase in activity and a growth in numbers. There may very well come a time when we are not personally involved in everything that goes on in our church. We must be willing to accept this and realize that a ministry of the church does not have to be important to *us* to be important. Just because we can do without a ministry personally does not mean our *church* can do without that ministry.

A HOMEY ATMOSPHERE

A woman new to our church came to me one day and said she understood why we used the slogan "Welcome to the Church of the Nazarene—Our Church Can Be Your Home," for this church truly had a homey atmosphere. All small-town churches, with God's help, should have an all-inclusive, homey atmosphere.

* * *

An Exercise Toward Revitalization

Answer the following questions:

1. Why would anyone choose your church to be his or her church home?

2. What things can be done to make your church more inviting to people looking for a church home?

12

Create Community Visibility

Let your light so shine before men,
that they may see your good works,
and glorify your Father which is in
heaven.
Matt. 5:16

The small-town church should be a vital part of its community. We have much to add to the atmosphere, attitude, and appearance of the communities in which we are situated. In many cases we have the opportunity to become a community church. But this will never happen until we become a church that is visible to our community. An essential step in the process of revitalizing the small-town church is to create community visibility. We need to be a church with a positive image in our community and a church with a high saturation level, always before the community.

VISIBLE PERSONNEL

The pastor of the small-town church must be a people person. It is essential to his personal ministry and the church's ministry that he has a high level of visibility within the community. He must be a man who still makes house calls. There is no substitute for the personal interest that is displayed in a pastor's house call. In addition to calling in the homes of his own people, he should also be willing to visit in the homes of others when an interest is expressed either personally or through a member of the church family.

He should have an active role in the local ministerial association. I have attended some ministerial association meetings that have been like going to church, and others in which I felt like a fish out of water. Whether the ministerial meeting is beneficial or not, it is an essential part of the responsibility of a small-town pastor.

For the small-town pastor, time spent in the coffee shops of his community is time well spent. He will be able to establish some valuable contacts around their tables.

A pastor should make all major community functions and school functions a very important part of his social calendar. He should show a personal interest in the young people and their activities. There is never any substitute for genuine interest and true concern for people. The pastor must know his community and be known by it.

Laypersons are also vital to their church's visibility. Laypersons, are you known for your close walk with Christ? Are the people of your community aware of your church affiliation? If you are who God wants you to be, then you are the best possible advertisement for your church. Good, strong Christian laypersons are the strongest drawing card of any church.

Vital Publicity

The local community newspaper is one of the best tools available to the small-town church in its effort to become visible in its community. If a local newspaper is available, whether weekly or daily, churches can use it to their advantage. In LaMoure, our paper is published weekly, but most of our ideas can be used as well in a daily paper.

Church Page Listing. The church schedule should be regularly included with a listing on the church page. All the essential ministries of the church should be included, along with the correct service times and the current pastor's name.

Promotional Articles. Most community newspapers will publish these articles free of charge. It is best if they are typed double-spaced on an 8½" x 11" sheet of paper. All special activities and ministries of the church can be promoted in this way. There are two tremendous benefits received through this means. First, it may bring people into the church for a special activity or service who otherwise would never have known it was taking place. Second, it will keep the name and ministries of the church before the community. It will be a constant reminder that the church is alive and well. We strive to have at least one promotional article in our paper each month.

Devotional Ads. One year our church put a monthly devotional ad in our paper. It was paid advertising and covered 8" or 9" of a single column. The ad featured a devotional thought from the pastor focusing on seasonal emphases, highlights of recent sermons, or thoughts on familiar scriptures. This gave our community a glimpse of the message of our church. We received many favorable comments from members of our community.

Advertisement Fliers. Fliers can be placed in each copy of the paper at a charge per copy. We have found this to be an especially good way to promote Vacation Bible School and other special children's emphases.

Special Ads. Once a year our newspaper publishes a special edition that is mailed to every resident countywide. It is our policy to run a quarter-page general ad in that edition, featuring a letter from the pastor and a list of ministries available through our church. If possible, it is also wise to place additional special ads in the paper quarterly.

Personal Congratulations. Our church is currently looking into the cost and feasibility of using the purchased newspaper for this purpose. Each week the small-town newspaper has many personal reports. Laminated copies of birth, wedding, and achievement announcements with an accompanying congratulatory letter from the pastor is another way the church can show its interest in the people of the community.

Radio and television afford other effective channels of publicity.

Public Service Announcements. Most radio stations and many television stations provide free publicity items received as public service announcements and/or community calendar items.

Devotionals. At the present time I have the opportunity of sharing a week's worth of devotional minutes on an area radio station. This is sponsored by the station and the local ministerial associations. Some stations will offer rates reasonable enough for a church to provide these on a daily basis.

Advertisements. Many of our churches are beginning to advertise regularly on the radio or television. This is another means to keep ourselves before the people of our community.

Christian radio provides a special opportunity and challenge.

Public Service Announcements. As in secular radio, most Christian radio stations provide free publication of items received as public service announcements or community calendar items.

Sponsorship. Our area's Christian radio station is commercial free. In each of the last two years, our church has sponsored a day's broadcast of the station's ministry.

Radio Rally. We have also had personnel from our area's Christian station come to our church to provide a

Sunday evening service of ministry and information concerning their program and ministry. This is mutually beneficial to the local small-town church and to the radio station.

COMMUNITY CANVAS

A community canvas, involving personal contact with every home in the community, should be made at least once every two years. There are two suggested ways in which this can be done.

Telemarketing. The telephone is a tool often neglected by the church. This type of approach can be used to conduct a simple survey to locate persons who may be interested in receiving more information about the church. It can also be used to invite the community to a special activity being planned by the church. In using the telephone, remember to keep your message simple, short, and sweet.

Door-to-door Literature Distribution. A few years ago, our church put together a package of literature describing our ministries and distributed it to every home in the community. The packet included a copy of the *Herald of Holiness,* a letter from the pastor, a special-edition newsletter, and a church theme card. Although this in itself, did not bring in any new people, it added to our community's awareness of who we are.

Contacting new neighbors is a beneficial task. Find a source of information that will enable you to know when new people move into the community. Members may visit their homes with homemade baked goods, literature concerning the church, and an invitation to services.

Many small-town schools are still willing to work with the churches of their community. We are able to do two specific things with our school. In March 1989, a blind pastor friend, Rev. O. Keith Bundy, was with our church for revival services. During that week we were able to get him into every class between kindergarten and sixth grade to share how he deals with blindness. His presentation included a short reading from his braille Bible, a demonstration of some of the equipment that is available to him, sharing from his personal experience, and an interesting question-and-answer time. Rev. Bundy also inscribed each of the students' names in braille on index cards, which he then gave to the students as a keepsake. Through our evangelist, our church was able to offer a worthwhile service to the community free of charge.

Later that same spring, we invited our high school to present its one-act play in our Sunday evening service. A few of the individuals involved in the play were from our church, and the play was very appropriate for a Sunday evening service.

Here are a few suggestions about other worthwhile ideas for publicity.

Church Signs. Every church needs signs located on the main thoroughfares of the community, directing people to its location. Every church also needs a sign on the property identifying the congregation and listing service times.

Posters, etc. Most small towns have various businesses in the community willing to display posters or fliers of coming events. This service should be used advantageously whenever possible.

Telephone Book Listing. Every church should have a listing of some sort in the white and yellow pages of the phone book. It makes the church more accessible to its community and to those who are passing through.

Community Church Services. If a community has joint services during the year, all churches should cooperate and participate in these services if at all possible. The small-town church must be a community-oriented church and must try to avoid being labeled as separatist.

* * *

An Exercise Toward Revitalization

A Visibility Test

Are you willing to put your church's visibility under scrutiny? If you are, I would like to give you a couple of suggestions.

1. The next time you have an out-of-town friend coming, have him stop at several businesses in your community to ask directions to your church.

2. For more information, conduct a survey asking members of your community to do the following.

    a. Name the pastor of your church.

    b. Name anyone they know who attends your church.

    c. Share anything they know about your church.

    d. Give their opinion of what benefit your church is to the community.

13

Identify Ministries with Potential for Outreach

Say not ye, There are yet four months, and then cometh harvest? behold, I say unto you, Lift up your eyes, and look on the fields; for they are white already to harvest. And he that reapeth receiveth wages, and gathereth fruit unto life eternal: that both he that soweth and he that reapeth may rejoice together. And herein is that saying true, One soweth, and another reapeth. I sent you to reap that whereon ye bestowed no labour: other men laboured, and ye are entered into their labours.

John 4:35-38

Enhanced activity increases the potential of the small-town church. Every ministry of the church serves as a new door from the community into the church. The more doors we are able to create, the more ways we are providing for people to enter the church. The philosophy of our local congregation is that any ministry that reaches one new person is a worthwhile outreach tool. Some of these ministries may already be a part of a particular church's program, while others will need to be added.

WEEKNIGHT CHILDREN'S MINISTRIES

There are three suggested options for a weeknight children's ministry in the local church. Which one is used may depend upon personnel, budget, and facilities. At one time our church had a Caravan program. We disbanded our Caravan in favor of an alternative program, CHOW (Children's Hour On Wednesday), because we lacked sufficient personnel to carry out a successful Caravan program. Although Caravan is beyond our capabilities at this time, a weeknight children's ministry is required, because through this ministry we are reaching children whom we are not reaching at any other time. Disbanding Caravan at this time was necessary, but disbanding a weeknight children's ministry was *not* an option.

Caravan. A Christian scouting program sponsored by the Church of the Nazarene, Caravan provides enjoyable and educational ways of facilitating spiritual, mental, physical, and social growth. There are badges, etc., to be earned, and it is a wonderful program. Supplies and materials are available through the Nazarene Publishing House. Information on how to start a Caravan is available through the Children's Ministries Office at the international headquarters of the Church of the Nazarene in Kansas City.

Caravan Sundays. As an extension of our church's Caravan ministry, four times a year we have provided an opportunity for the Caravan children to share with the congregation what they have been doing. It has also brought the Caravaners and their families into our church for a special Sunday morning service.

Kids for Christ Club. Grade schoolers will come to a Christian club for children featuring music, story time, crafts, refreshments, and Scripture memorization. This type of program worked very well in one particular church. It does not require a lot of adult supervision, and it is a fun time of learning for the children involved.

CHOW (Children's Hour On Wednesday). A weeknight children's ministry, CHOW provides the children with an opportunity to learn many things. We have had lots of "hands-on" activities such as a section on the "Bee-attitudes," lambing, wheat grinding, a visit to a bird sanctuary, and many others. Special guests have shared with the kids what they do on their farms, in their businesses, etc., with follow-up field trips to these places to actually see how things operate. We have also used this time to prepare children's musicals and study the quizzing material. CHOW is a little less structured than Caravan and requires fewer people to staff it, but it can be every bit as exciting and informative.

CHOW Down. Special Sundays have replaced the Caravan Sundays in our local program. Like the Caravan Sundays, they have been held approximately four times a year. They have featured musicals, Scripture memorization, sharing our learning experiences, choruses, and many other activities. This will still provide opportunity for the children to acquaint the congregation and their parents with the CHOW program.

T-N-T Power Club. A new program to us, the Power Club meets Wednesdays for a couple of hours after school. It is designed to be a reach-out opportunity for the children of our community. On the first Wednesday afternoon of the month, the lesson is taken from the Children's Missions Packet, and the story, activities, and review games center around the information found there. The second and fourth Wednesday afternoons are used for Bible study. The Bible lesson is taught with a flannelgraph, using the Scripture lesson from the children's quizzing material. The scripture memorization is from scriptures that are required learning from the quizzing material. The review games are made up of the questions in the quizzing books but are presented in such a way that it does not seem like bookwork, but rather a fun way to learn material.

The third Wednesday afternoon of the month is designated as Activity Night. This varies from month to month. Some activities for this night are crafts, field trips, special speakers, and historical programs available from our State Heritage Center. Any fifth Wednesday is Celebration Day and takes the place of our Children's Saturdays. These are used for seasonal parties and other activities and also help free up those Saturdays throughout the year.

T-N-T Hour of Power. An equivalent to a Caravan Sunday or CHOW Down. It is a way to share with the parents of those involved in T-N-T Power Club what we do each week in this ministry. These special Sundays are also held approximately four times a year.

Vacation Bible School. In most of our small-town churches, Vacation Bible School is a long-standing tradition; but there are various approaches to VBS. In many churches, it is something they do for their own kids. They are sometimes afraid it will become a baby-sitting service if opened up to the entire community. Besides, it might prove to be more than can be handled and it might cost too much money.

Our Vacation Bible School though is definitely a community event. We schedule it after all the other Vacation Bible Schools are over. We draw unchurched children and children from every church in town as well as our own. It is full of fun and excitement, complete with clowns, puppets, songs, stories, crafts, Bible stories, and memory verses. The children receive the gospel message and are glad they do. It is a great ministry we provide for any and all the children in our community, and God is using our willingness for His glory.

Children's Saturdays. Special days are held between four and six times a year and will last anywhere from two to eight hours, depending upon the scheduled activities.

These Saturdays are geared for the children who are involved in our Sunday School, CHOW, and Vacation Bible School. These activities are the only official contact we have with some children between Vacation Bible Schools. Children's Saturdays activities have included a birthday party for Jesus in December, an Easter egg hunt in the spring, a Vacation Bible School picnic in the summer, and at least one special out-of-town trip each year.

SAM (Senior Adult Ministries). At the present time our SAM consists of fellowship dinners held approximately every other month. A large percentage of our community is aged 55 and older, so this could become a great outreach tool as it continues and develops.

LIFT (Ladies' Inspirational Fellowship Time). A group of ladies meets monthly for a time of wonderful fellowship, devotions, and some type of program. From time to time they also take on special projects. This group is proving their effectiveness as a tool of outreach ministry.

NYI (Nazarene Youth International). The church's ministry to youth should be a well-balanced program. A successful youth ministry program has a balance between (1) fun and fellowship, (2) discipleship and worship, and (3) ministry and missions. Each of these three categories is an essential part of success in ministering to today's youth.

Men of the Nazarene. Most churches lack any kind of strong men's organization. We are currently working on the establishment of such a group in our church. We envision this ministry to include a breakfast once or twice a year with a special speaker, a weekly men's prayer time (which is already a part of our church's program), occasional fellowships, group trips, at least one father-son activity a year, and a work project in a district home missions church.

Nursing Home Ministry. For the past 15 years a layman from our church has provided a weekly Bible study in our local nursing home. This has been a ministry treasured by the residents and appreciated throughout the community. In addition to the residents, we often have visitors from the various churches of our community in attendance. The service usually consists of singing, prayer, and Bible study. Other ministries we provide at the nursing home include Christmas cantatas, small-group Bible studies, and chapel with our pastor once every six weeks. Once or twice a year, our ladies provide the nursing home birthday party.

SPECIAL SUNDAY EVENING PRESENTATIONS

Films. Many of the Billy Graham films are now available on a freewill offering basis. These serve as a great tool for an outreach service. Other videos and films may also be rented to show on a Sunday evening.

Concerts. Area groups, Nazarene song evangelists, and groups from our colleges may be available to hold a concert on Sunday or on a weeknight. These, too, are great opportunities for outreach.

Cantatas. We are privileged in our church to have one of the finest small-church choirs anywhere. At least twice a year our choir presents a special program of music in the Sunday evening service. Churches without a choir can use whatever music is available, for music can be a great drawing card.

Dramatizations. A couple of Sunday evenings a year the pastor will do a biblical character dramatization in the Sunday evening service.

BANQUETS

Each of these banquet-type events provides a great opportunity to invite a friend from outside the regular church family.

Valentine Banquet. An activity for our adults, this occasion for remembering is held each year in one of our community restaurants. It is an evening with fun and games, fabulous food, wonderful fellowship, music, and a devotional. Some years we invite a special speaker and musician, while other years we take care of this ourselves.

Mother-Daughter Banquet. A particularly special event is held annually in our church's fellowship hall. For the past four years this banquet has featured the pastor as chef, and the men of the church have served the meal and washed the dishes. A special speaker and music have been brought in from other churches.

Father-Son Cookout. An informal gathering at the park features food and games and a devotional. One of the hardest activities to arrange, it is, however, one of the most enjoyable to experience.

THE USE OF SPECIAL SUNDAYS

Mothers' and Fathers' Day Services. In most of our churches special days to honor our parents have been celebrated annually with a service planned along an appropriate theme. However, have we promoted these special days in our communities at large? They are golden opportunities for outreach.

Teen, Children, and Baby Day Services. Every church should plan a special day during the year to recognize the youth of the church. Each of these days provide opportunities for both outreach and highlighting our young people. Baby Day parade is a delight to all.

Sweetheart Sunday. In either October or February a time should be set aside to recognize married couples and emphasize the sanctity of marriage.

Senior Citizens' and Grandparents' Appreciation Sunday. Each September, to the best of our ability, invitations are sent to every senior citizen in our community. Every senior citizen and grandparent present is recognized in the special morning worship service, and a dinner is held in their honor in the fellowship hall after the service. This is always one of our best-attended services of the year.

Veterans and Military Personnel Appreciation Sunday. A service to honor our armed forces personnel, held in November, has proved to be another high point in our church year. Letters of personal invitation are sent by the pastor to every veteran and member of the military residing in our community. This past year the service included a Coast Guard color guard, patriotic music, the recognition of all present and former military personnel, an appropriate message from God's Word by the pastor, and a dinner in honor of the veterans and military personnel in the fellowship hall following the service. After the first of these services, there was a special thank-you note in the classified section of our newspaper, placed by our local veterans' organization.

Public School Staff Appreciation Sunday. Still another high point in the ministry of the church has been a special service, held in May, to honor our public school teachers. We have tried various programs for this day, such as a children's musical and a film geared toward teachers. We have served dinner following the morning service on two occasions, and a continental breakfast before the morning service on another. This emphasis has been very well received and much appreciated by the staff of our school.

Health Care Givers' Sunday. Another well-received special day honors medical burden-bearers. Invitations are sent to every health care employee in our county, including nursing home staff, clinic staff, and ambulance squad members. Each of these individuals is recognized in the service and dinner is served following the service.

Service Club Sundays. Each of our communities has service clubs, which perform valuable service projects for the community. One of these organizations and their members could be honored in one of the church services. We honored the Lions Club for their service to the visually impaired on the Sunday we had a blind evangelist. That evening two lawyers in our community were in attendance for the final service of our revival meeting.

The list could go on and on: Community Day, Homecoming, "Laborers for Jesus" Sunday, Community Leaders' Sunday, Little League Sunday, Girl Scout and Boy Scout Sundays—to name just a few. The possibilities are endless. Each church may dream up even more ideas of its own.

*   *   *

An Exercise Toward Revitalization

1. What "doors" are there leading into your church at this time?

2. What "doors" could be created to bring new people into your church?

14

Keep Your Denominational Identity

Give unto the Lord the glory due unto his name: bring an offering, and come before him: worship the Lord in the beauty of holiness.

1 Chron. 16:29

It is possible to keep your denominational identity while revitalizing the small-town church. It is possible to become a community church without diminishing your denominational identity. Some small-town churches fail to be revitalized because they are afraid their church will lose its spiritual identity. They are fearful of losing their doctrinal distinction by bringing into the church family people with no previous church affiliation or differing church affiliation.

While this is always possible, it does not have to be the case. There are things that can be done to help a church maintain its denominational identity while adding to its numbers.

A church does not have to water down its message to appeal to the new people coming through the doors. Our message of holiness is relevant to this day. People coming to us are looking for God, and we must have the courage to preach the total Word of God. I believe in scriptural holiness, and I preach it more now than ever before.

Here are ways to keep denominational identity in periods of church growth.

ATTEND DENOMINATIONAL ACTIVITIES

Each quadrennium there are several activities scheduled by the denomination, which are beneficial to all small-town pastors. If possible, the pastor should attend all of these. If this is not possible, he should attend at least one each quadrennium. These activities include General Conventions and Assembly, PALCON (Pastors And Leaders Conference), Evangelism Conference, and regional missionary workshops.

Each year there are also many district activities. The small-town pastor should attend each of these activities unless providentially hindered. These would include District Assembly, NWMS Convention, NYI Convention, Sunday School Ministries Convention, pastors' seminars, Pastors' and Wives' Retreat, and Camp Meeting. A pastor should also counsel at one district youth camp a year if possible and be willing to serve in any district position to which he is elected or appointed.

Each month the pastors of each zone should meet together for a time of fellowship and interaction. These various connections between the small-town pastor and his denomination will strengthen the ties between the local church and its denomination as well.

The laity of the church should be encouraged to get involved in at least some of these services. As many persons as possible should attend at least one district function a year. These functions include district conventions and assemblies, camp meetings, youth camps and retreats, lay retreats, women's retreats, and singles' retreats, to name a few. If possible, at least one all-church trip to the church's regional college campus should be planned each quadrennium.

Bring in Denominational Leaders

Understanding that it is never possible to get all people to a district or denominational function, it is beneficial when a district or denominational leader can be brought into the local church. These include the district superintendent and his wife, international headquarters leaders, evangelists, and missionaries. In the fall of 1989, we were privileged to have Dr. Orville Jenkins, general superintendent emeritus, in our church for revival. The benefits of that revival have been far-reaching. Not only was the Lord able to use him to bring souls into the Kingdom and draw others closer to God, but also it helped some of our new people feel the heartbeat of our denomination.

Use Denominational Materials

The materials produced by the Nazarene Publishing House are second to none. They are excellent for use during Sunday School and adult Bible study, other small-group Bible study meetings, the monthly NWMS meetings, and the weekly NYI meetings. Other materials available include CLT (Continuing Lay Training) courses, which can be used during Wednesday night prayer meeting or other nights of the week, and Bible studies.

Promote Denominational Periodicals

It is beneficial to get denominational periodicals into the homes of our people, including Sunday School papers, the *Come Ye Apart* devotional book, and the *Herald of Holiness* magazine. Our promotion of the *Herald of Holiness* is quite comprehensive. One year this included the hanging of a poster in the foyer, the setup of a special display on a table in the foyer, and the distribution of available wrapped copies of the *Herald* to every family of the church. We also took time in a morning worship service for each family who was not currently receiving the *Herald* to fill out a coupon for three months of the *Herald,* which they received free of charge.

PARTICIPATE IN SPECIAL OFFERINGS

It is important for our people to give to each special denominational offering. It is equally vital to reinform them of the purpose of those offerings. We have used videos available through Nazarene Publishing House, or skits during morning worship services, to inform the people who are new to our church of the purposes of these special offerings. These offerings include Alabaster, World Mission Radio, Thanksgiving and Easter Offerings for World Missions, Hunger and Disaster Fund, Compassionate Ministries Offering, and offerings for Nazarene Bible College and Nazarene Theological Seminary.

PRESENT DENOMINATIONAL THEMES LOCALLY

It was a privilege to attend the 1989 General Conventions and Assembly in Indianapolis. A highlight of those meetings was the quadrennial theme presentations. Unfortunately, my family and I were the only people from our local church in attendance. We decided to bring a little of their flavor to the local church. Since our return from those meetings, we have adapted those presentations and have used them in our local church. We also plan to do this annually with the district theme presentations. Whenever our people cannot go to the general church, let us make every effort to bring the general church to our people. This includes a time for sharing about any district or general function from which any of the church's people have just returned.

MEMBERSHIP CLASS

A membership class is a must for all prospective members and a plus for everyone. At least once a year the pastor or a layman should conduct a membership class for anyone interested in church membership and everyone who is new to the church. This class can be conducted during the Sunday School hour or on a special evening during the week. There are many great resources available through our publishing house. The newest and one of the best of these is *Welcome to the Church of the Nazarene: An Introduction to Membership,* by Dr. Richard Parrott.

In addition to this class, I have found it helpful to present these materials for a month on Sunday nights. This not only reaches our new people but also gives our long-time members and attenders a refresher course. The first time we tried this approach, we had someone come in from the community to learn more about our church. This person is now an active member of our congregation.

TOPICAL BIBLE STUDIES

Once each quadrennium we have done a topical study of the Articles of Faith in our Wednesday evening prayer meeting and Bible study. We usually deal with one article of faith a night and cover them quite comprehensively. I would also recommend that a catechism class on the Articles of Faith be offered to the junior class in the Children's Department once every three years.

Not only is it possible to keep one's denominational identity, but it is important and necessary. Without denigrating other denominations, we need to busy ourselves in fulfilling the purpose of God in raising up our own church.

* * *

An Exercise Toward Revitalization

1. List both the privileges and the responsibilities of being part of a denomination, both to you personally and to your local church.

2. List all the things you can think of that have connected your local church with your denomination in the last year.

3. List all the things you can think of that have connected your local church with your denomination in the last three years.

Conclusion

The process for revitalizing the church set forth in the preceding pages is not a theory developed in a sterilized and controlled environment. It is a formula developed in the always-changing world of the small-town church. Theories have not been ignored—they have been put to work.

The success of this formula for local churches will not be found through a rigid adherence to our process but by grasping its purposes and principles. It is not necessary that another church do everything just as we have done it. Feel free to adopt anything that can be used, adapt anything as needed, add anything that is helpful, and delete anything that does not apply.

This formula is by nature a process. The ideas presented here were not the result of one day's work or one evening's board meeting. They have been developed at a steady pace, one or two ideas at a time, over a period of five years. Even now it is not complete but remains a continuing process. Our attitudinal approach is not to get it over and done with, but rather, to keep at the task of revitalizing the church. The work of the church must go on.

The story of what God is doing in the LaMoure Church of the Nazarene is not magical—it is miraculous. It is the story of what can happen when pastor, people, and God come together to form an unbeatable team.

It is our hope that this work will be an encouragement to all churches and a discouragement to none.

Augustine said, "Without God we cannot, and without us He will not." May we each be about the task of revitalizing the church to His glory. Never say, "Never," for with God all things are possible.

Notes

Chapter 1

1. C. Peter Wagner, *Leading Your Church to Growth* (Ventura, Calif.: Regal Books, 1984), 17.

2. Robert H. Schuller, *Your Church Has a Fantastic Future* (Ventura, Calif.: Regal Books, 1986), 292.

3. Bernard Quiun et al., *Churches and Church Membership in the United States, 1980* (Atlanta: Glenmary Research Center, 1980), 211.

4. C. Peter Wagner, "Must a Healthy Church Be a Growing Church?" *Leadership* 2, no. 1 (Winter 1981): 128.

Chapter 4

1. Statistics from Church Growth Division, Church of the Nazarene, Kansas City.

Chapter 6

1. Information available through the United States Census Bureau and the Church Growth Division, Church of the Nazarene, Kansas City.